MOUNTAINTOP MINING IN APPALACHIA

STUDIES IN CONFLICT, JUSTICE, AND SOCIAL CHANGE

Series Editors: Susan F. Hirsch and Agnieszka Paczyńska

This series is funded in part through the generous support of the School for Conflict Analysis and Resolution at George Mason University.

Susan F. Hirsch and E. Franklin Dukes, *Mountaintop Mining in Appalachia: Understanding Stakeholders and Change in Environmental Conflict*

MOUNTAINTOP MINING IN APPALACHIA

Understanding Stakeholders and Change in Environmental Conflict

SUSAN F. HIRSCH AND E. FRANKLIN DUKES

OHIO UNIVERSITY PRESS, ATHENS

Ohio University Press, Athens, Ohio 45701
ohioswallow.com
© 2014 by Ohio University Press
All rights reserved

To obtain permission to quote, reprint, or otherwise reproduce or distribute material
from Ohio University Press publications, please contact our rights and permissions
department at (740) 593-1154 or (740) 593-4536 (fax).

Printed in the United States of America
Ohio University Press books are printed on acid-free paper ∞ ™

24 23 22 21 20 19 18 17 16 15 14   5 4 3 2 1

Library of Congress Cataloging-in-Publication Data
Hirsch, Susan F.
 Mountaintop mining in Appalachia : understanding stakeholders and change in
environmental conflict / Susan F. Hirsch and E. Franklin Dukes.
    pages cm — (Studies in conflict, justice, and social change)
 Includes bibliographical references and index.
 ISBN 978-0-8214-2109-3 (hardback) — ISBN 978-0-8214-2110-9 (paperback) — ISBN
978-0-8214-4509-9 (electronic)
 1. Mountaintop removal mining—Environmental aspects—Appalachian Region. 2.
Environmental policy—Appalachian Region. 3. Environmentalism—Appalachian
Region. 4. Mountaintop removal mining—Government policy—Appalachian Region.
5. Mountaintop removal mining—Social aspects—Appalachian Region. 6. Coal mines
and mining—Environmental aspects—Appalachian Region. 7. Appalachian Region—
Environmental conditions. I. Dukes, E. Franklin. II. Title.
 TD195.C58H57 2014
 333.8'220974—dc23

                    2014023684

To everyone who
works to create and
sustain a place
they call home.

CONTENTS

ILLUSTRATIONS

Figures

Map

ACKNOWLEDGMENTS

Mountaintop mining, and the conflict over the practice, affects many people in profound ways. For this book, which seeks to explain how stakeholders experience this issue, we have relied on the help of many individuals who are involved firsthand in the situation. We acknowledge with appreciation the generosity and candor of people—from activists to regulators to industry personnel to educators to community leaders—who spoke to us about their involvement in the conflict over mountaintop mining. We are especially grateful to have spoken with many residents of the coal-producing region and learned about their lives and concerns. We choose not to identify by name the many people with whom we interacted while working on this project; however, we remember Larry Gibson and Judy Bonds, who were generous in sharing their perspectives. We also thank the many participants in the Clinch River Valley Initiative (CRVI), featured in chapter 5, and Frank's CRVI cofacilitator, Christine Gyovai.

We benefited from students, colleagues, family members, and friends who helped with the research and editing of the book, including Maria Dolores Rodriguez, Gina Cerasani, Caroline Sarkis, Derek Sweetman, and the Writing Guild, a group of faculty and graduate students at George Mason University. Thanks to Michael English for careful preparation of the index. Agnieszka Paczynska, coeditor of the series in which this book appears, made excellent editorial suggestions. Michael Sullivan provided both technical and editorial advice, as well as invaluable support. Jim Lance shepherded the project in its early days. Working with Gillian Berchowitz in her capacity as director of Ohio University Press has been delightful and rewarding, and the press staff and copyeditor have made publication a smooth process. Finally, we are also grateful for support from the School for Conflict Analysis and Resolution at George Mason University and the Institute for Environmental Negotiation at the University of Virginia.

ABBREVIATIONS

CAFHP   Central Appalachia Food Heritage Project
CRMW   Coal River Mountain Watch
CRVI   Clinch River Valley Initiative
CWA   Clean Water Act of 1972
EIS   Environmental Impact Statement
FACES [of Coal]   Federation for American Coal, Energy and Security
IEN   Institute for Environmental Negotiation, University
                      of Virginia
MJS   Mountain Justice Summer
MSHA   Mine Safety and Health Academy
MTM   mountaintop mining
MTR   mountaintop removal mining
NWP 21   Nationwide Permit 21
SMCRA   Surface Mining Control and Reclamation Act of 1977
SOAR   Shaping Our Appalachian Region
TNC   The Nature Conservancy
USACE   US Army Corps of Engineers
VNRLI   Virginia Natural Resources Leadership Institute
WVCA   West Virginia Coal Association

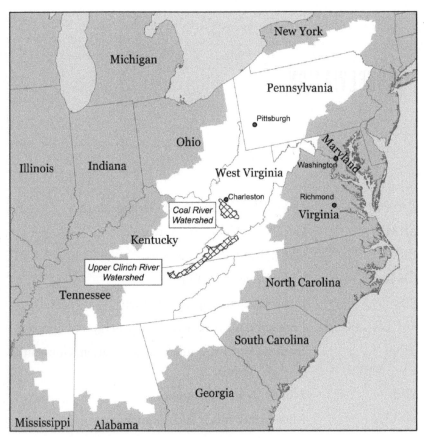

Areas in Appalachia profiled for this book. *Tad Slawecki.*

ONE

Introduction

The Bands Play On

As the band finished its last song on Labor Day 2009, couples reluctantly turned toward their cars. Many families had already returned home to put tired kids to bed. Rock-legend-turned-hunter-and-conservative-icon Ted Nugent and his band had blasted familiar music as the final act of an all-day concert on a large field—once the site of a surface mine—in southwestern West Virginia. The free concert, which had also featured Hank Williams Jr., provided welcome entertainment for the crowd of mostly coal miners and their families. Despite the blistering heat of the late summer day, they had rocked to the music and enjoyed eating barbecue and drinking cold beer and soft drinks from the food stands. Some wore shirts bearing the name of their mining company or the increasingly popular Friends of Coal logo. Concert organizers called the afternoon of performances and speeches the Friends of America rally, and it proved to be a welcome diversion for these working people.

Mining coal in Appalachia is not an easy way to make a living. Miners daily face the threat of injury or worse, and the mining industry's apparently increasing vulnerability to economic competition and environmental concerns in an unstable economy creates anxiety for everyone. Many people attending the concert came from families in which men had proudly made their living mining coal for several generations. By sponsoring the rally, the coal companies were not only demonstrating their generosity but also showing miners that they counted on their loyalty, and many miners believed in the message—shouted out by Ted Nugent—that the coal industry would provide them with jobs for a long time (Cooper 2009).

Earlier that same summer, a different group of people gathered not far away, in North Carolina, to enjoy music. In coming together, their goal was to support the movement against a type of surface coal mining sometimes known as mountaintop removal mining (MTR). Concert attendees came from across the United States and included young people who had traveled to the region for the summer to support local anti-MTR activists. Many in the audience were Appalachians of diverse ages and backgrounds who had concerns about the impacts to their communities from MTR. Together, they danced and sang to the strains of country music, folk, and rock interspersed with speeches designed to fire them up for more action against the MTR side of the coal industry.

Country music star Kathy Mattea not only wowed the crowd with her vocals but urged those present to work against MTR. Banners and T-shirts displayed names of the many organizations that had long sought to draw attention to controversial coal-mining practices, including Ohio Valley Environmental Coalition, Kentuckians for the Commonwealth, Sierra Club, and Southern Appalachian Mountain Stewards. Everyone enjoyed socializing that day, and organizers hoped to raise enough money to help relocate a West Virginia school sitting directly downstream from an earthen dam holding back millions of gallons of mine waste. Although the fight against MTR had been going on for years, and mining had consumed ever larger areas of West Virginia, Virginia, and Kentucky, those who opposed MTR sensed that their issue was on the verge of gaining the attention and sympathy of a national audience (HuntingtonNews 2009).

Before and after both concerts, individuals representing these starkly distinct perspectives—those who support MTR and those who oppose it—had confronted one another face to face on many different occasions. Whenever they did, tensions ran high. Many times violence threatened to break out and sometimes it did. In some instances—for example, at a hearing over whether a coal company should receive a permit for MTR—those attending were well aware not only of the tension but also that the future of coal mining in the region was at stake (Ward 2009).

Coal miners and anti-MTR activists are two major categories of stakeholder in the large and complex conflict over mining in Appalachia. In describing them and the many other stakeholders from the perspective of the conflict field, this book offers a window into the conflict over a form of surface mining that gives rise to one of the most significant environmental conflicts in the United States.

Before we can begin to write about stakeholders and the conflict over mining practices, we need to explore the use of language in writing about these issues. Our intent in this book is not to favor any particular perspective but to present those divergent perspectives in ways that help the reader understand what is at stake for different people and why they act as they do. But the use of language is itself an element of the conflict, and our choice of vocabulary may attract or alienate different stakeholders despite our intentions.

For instance, *coalfields* is a common term for the location in Appalachia where coal mining has historically taken place. Some residents use that term with pride. But other residents reject the term, arguing that it implies that coal mining is the only activity worth featuring in a region with many other dimensions. In this book, we generally use the term *coalfields* only in referencing situations where the stakeholders themselves do so. We refer instead to Appalachia, knowing too that this geographic reference also has a contested history (see, e.g., Biggers 2006).

Until now we have called the conflict a conflict over mountaintop removal mining, but even the name of the practice is controversial. Coal producers and some community advocates reject the label MTR, as it focuses on the negative idea of removal rather than on mining, which has economic and other, more favorable, connotations. They prefer the more general phrase *surface mining*. Other environmental advocates believe that *surface mining* is a deceptive term because it fails to mention one of its most significant problems: the destruction of mountaintops. From this point forward, while acknowledging that others prefer different terms, we use the phrase *mountaintop mining* (MTM) because we believe it is both descriptive of the practice and less tainted by the perception of partiality.

Mountaintop Mining and Environmental Conflicts

The issues related to mountaintop mining have their own particular origins and dynamics and their own sets of stakeholders. But similar issues characterize other environmental conflicts, and similarities also exist in the interactions among stakeholders. Environmental conflicts are ubiquitous, complex, and enduring. They represent a considerable financial and social drain on communities. These conflicts also help shape, and in turn are shaped by, foundational issues such as human well-being, ecosystem health, and the viability of human communities.

Conflicts in the environmental arena invoke passion and controversy throughout the world, partly because they involve competition between the provision of fundamental human needs for clean air and water and uncontaminated land, on the one hand, and economic sustenance and development, on the other. But the intensity of many environmental conflicts also derives from competing visions of, and claims to, individual and community identity.

Those identity issues are significant in MTM, and we explore them throughout this book. But the sheer scale of environmental and economic considerations related to MTM are also staggering. Hundreds of thousands of acres of land are being altered dramatically, with the tops of mountains literally blown away, and hundreds of miles of streams filled or contaminated. At the same time, hundreds of millions of dollars and thousands of jobs are at stake in a region where poverty and unemployment are endemic. For those seeking slogans, the competing calls to "Protect the environment" versus "Protect jobs" are simple ways to depict the conflict. But, as we will show, the reality of the MTM conflict is much more complex than any slogans might suggest.

The practice of MTM has deeply divided Appalachian communities. While community and environmental activists fight to end it, mining companies, miners, and other community activists fight to keep it going. This book is about that fight and, in particular, the efforts and experiences of the stakeholders directly and indirectly involved in it.

Why Is It Important to Understand MTM?

For those stakeholders who are directly involved in the conflict, nothing is more important than MTM. For those who have raised alarms about the practice of MTM, at stake are the safety and security of their homes, schools, and communities, as well as the heritage represented by the region's natural resources and mountain beauty. For those who work in the mining industry, at stake are employment, income, and identity as coal producers. For public officials in the region, at stake are concerns about economic development, a shrinking tax base, and potential hard times to come. And for all stakeholders, at stake is their identity: who gets to claim to be the people who care for their community, who work hard, who support their families, who protect their children, who prepare for the future, and who preserve their heritage.

For those who have little connection to MTM directly, or for whom questions of energy policy may not be of much interest, this issue nonetheless provides a compelling case study of challenges to democracy and governance. Who decides the future of a community, a region, a landscape, a river, a mine? Who benefits from any gain, and who is left out? What say does a community have when it faces irrevocable change, whether through MTM, efforts to outlaw MTM, or changes in the energy economy? Whose voices should be heard on this issue? What does it take for the voices of stakeholders to have an impact?

Organization of the Book

This book presents a complex conflict along with key concepts and theories from the field of conflict analysis and resolution. Analyzing any conflict may identify deep-rooted causes, which often go well beyond the surface issues that parties to a conflict articulate. Looking deeper can reveal causes that stand in the way of resolution, such as structural impediments in the form of institutions, politics, and inequality or the strongly held values of parties that find it difficult to resolve their differences. These causes are present in the conflict over MTM.

In this book we focus particularly on stakeholders, a central concept in the conflict field, and ask: Who considers themselves stakeholders in the MTM conflict? Who has not yet realized that they have a connection to MTM? What happens when people become aware that they have a stake in a conflict? What are stakeholders doing to overcome the impasse between supporters and opponents of MTM? Also of interest is that some people get involved in the MTM conflict out of concern for the environmental effects of mining, even though their own stake is less immediate than that of individuals who depend on mining for a job or who suffer its environmental impact directly. In this way the conflict over MTM is similar to other environmental conflicts, and thus the lessons learned about stakeholders in the MTM conflict are relevant to understanding many other conflicts over environmental issues.

Through the chapters that follow you will read about how this conflict has come to a head, assess the actions of some of the key stakeholders, and ponder the future of coal mining in two areas of southern Appalachia: southwestern West Virginia and southwestern Virginia (see Map). You'll find out that you, too, are a stakeholder in the conflict over mining in Appalachia. You might be challenged to consider whether you have a say in the conflict over MTM or whether you may have an impact on its future.

Chapter 2 provides a broad look at the conflict over mountaintop mining and maps out its central components. What are the actual practices of MTM, and why do they generate such conflict? What role do efforts to regulate MTM through state and federal branches of government play in the conflict? In fact, much of the MTM conflict centers on attempts by mining companies to acquire permits to mine and on efforts to prevent permits from being issued. These struggles over the regulation of coal mining involve institutions with home bases outside the coal-producing region, such as the US Army Corps of Engineers (USACE), the Environmental Protection Agency (EPA), and the Sierra Club, as well as other national environmental organizations.

Chapter 3 explains our approach to stakeholders. A simple definition of *stakeholder* is any person involved in, or affected by, a conflict. Our discussion presents multiple ways of understanding the stakeholder concept and applies that concept to the conflict over MTM. In this chapter you'll learn more about the two camps of stakeholders mentioned above, and you'll find out that a wide variety of other people, groups, and institutions are also stakeholders. Many stakeholders (for instance, politicians, coal operators, and energy consumers) were not present at the two music festivals described in the vignettes at the beginning of this chapter, nor at the tension-filled encounters over the years. In fact, millions of people are stakeholders in the conflict over whether and how to mine coal. If you live on the Eastern Seaboard of the United States, you might be a consumer of electricity from power plants that burn coal mined in Appalachia. If you live in another part of the country, the utility that provides your power may be operating in competition with Appalachian coal interests. If you live outside the United States, particularly in China, you may be using coal imported from the Appalachia region. In any of these cases you are a stakeholder, too.

Chapter 4 takes a closer look at the relationships among stakeholders and how they have shifted over the years as the conflict has developed, escalated, and changed. Different aspects of the stakeholder concept come alive as those involved pursue various strategies and tactics, including lawsuits, rallies, mediations, public discussions, and lots of behind-the-scenes activities. This chapter also addresses the threats and violence that have been inherent in the MTM conflict from the beginning. While violence, including that between stakeholders, is not new to the region, instances associated with the conflict have shocked residents and outsiders alike and raised fears of potential escalation. Also highlighted in the chapter are attempts to reduce and prevent violence using approaches from the conflict resolution field.

Throughout the conflict over MTM, productive discussions that bring together parties holding divergent perspectives on MTM have been few and far between. The deep divisions in the outlooks of stakeholders in the conflict, and the violence that has sometimes erupted, have stood in the way of dialogues, negotiations, visioning sessions, or just plain talk among stakeholders. Chapter 5 tells the story of one of the few attempts to engage stakeholders in a consensus-building project: the Clinch River Valley Initiative. The stakeholders who participated in the process have had profound experiences and have achieved significant goals, and the chapter concludes with an assessment of how consensus-building processes might be used more broadly in this and other environmental conflicts.

Chapter 6 returns to the struggle over how MTM is regulated, specifically exploring how legal actions ranging from lawsuits to legislation to federal and state regulations are intertwined with local, state, and national politics. For stakeholders, involvement in a highly politicized conflict has multiple consequences. For example, those stakeholders with little political or economic power might find it difficult to be heard or to have an impact. Yet even powerful parties, such as coal companies or national environmental organizations, seek the support of a wide range of stakeholders through advertising campaigns, films, and protests. Stakeholders always play key roles in the transformation of a conflict; however, many factors can lead to lasting and significant change.

The book's concluding chapter reviews the points made about the stakeholder concept and forecasts the future of the MTM conflict. The conclusion challenges you, as a reader, to consider your role as a stakeholder in the conflict and to determine what that might mean for your actions.

TWO

The Conflict over Mountaintop Mining

Through a maze of halls and shelves, we are led to the office of a stakeholder in the mountaintop-mining conflict. Our interview with Sim Ewing, vice-chancellor of the University of Virginia's College at Wise and a longtime civic leader, prompts reflection beyond his usual work. He notes that southwest Virginia has a long history of conflict over coal issues, a conflict that spills over into other arenas. Mining and its costs and benefits often permeate issues that one might expect would have nothing to do with coal. For example, the county we are in has lost population and tax revenue. The school system will soon be consolidating its high schools. The remaining schools will likely be located near the biggest population centers, so smaller coal communities are facing the loss of their schools, which means a loss of a key part of a community's identity. For people who live in these communities, it seems like a coal issue. Coal and money are being taken from their community, and now their schools are being taken, too.

Ewing muses about leadership in the region. People have a good work ethic and skills, but the general mindset is that they are a working class and that they report to someone; the area lacks the culture of initiative that is necessary for running one's own business. A small group of influential elites controls most boards and committees. There is real poverty and real wealth and not that much in between.

When asked what it would take to bring people together to talk about the issues involved in the conflicts over coal, he observes that these issues have been hundreds of years in the making. As in most communities, there is a general mistrust of outsiders, but residents give 110 percent to those whom they trust. Ideally, a long-term commitment to any effort at dialogue is important. Confirming others' opinion, he notes that the communities in the region are good at regional cooperation. But do regional projects mean too much time talking and not enough action? Smaller-scale projects can provide hope and set successful examples for others. Ewing closes by noting the tremendous potential in the area. The right project can really have a positive impact.

The Challenges of an Environmental Conflict

What makes for an intractable environmental conflict? Angry residents. Defensive industry. Undependable or unresponsive government agencies. Confusion and debates over scientific and technical information. Fears of permanent damage to landscapes and homes and entire communities. Credible rumors of loss of jobs and of ways of life. Protracted legal battles and threats of litigation. The conflict over MTM has all these features, which makes it similar to other environmental conflicts; they seem never to be over, as parties return for the next round of litigation, advocacy, or new development. Conflicts over environmental issues that involve community members, industry, localities, and federal and state agencies represent an enormous financial and social drain on communities and nations.

At stake in the most intractable environmental conflicts are such fundamental issues as individual and community health, justice for poor people or racial and ethnic minorities, the preservation or destruction of whole ecosystems, and the economic or cultural viability of various human communities. The arena of environmental conflict invokes so much passion because the consequences to individual and community well-being are so profound. It is not unusual for people engaged in an environmental conflict to claim that they are fighting so hard because they believe that the very survival of their neighborhood, livelihood, or planet is at stake.

As the global population grows, economic growth intensifies, and climate impacts increase, the pressure on natural, cultural, and historic resources becomes severe. Environmental issues offer particular challenges because of their impacts across communities and on multiple levels of governance. Conflict is often experienced within a community as well as between communities sharing the same resources, and also between responsible agencies of government with different missions. The involvement of so many diverse stakeholders at different societal levels makes environmental conflicts complex to understand and resistant to resolution.

A related challenge is the potential global scale of many environmental concerns. For instance, deforestation in the Amazon region can be linked not only to local and regional impacts, such as flooding, but also to global climate change and the world market for hardwood. For conflict analysts seeking to understand an environmental conflict holistically, attention has to be paid to the experiences of individuals close to the site of impact—such as an active mine, a forest slated for clear-cutting, a river about to be dammed—and also to the people across the contiguous region, the rest of the nation, and even across the globe who might feel its effects through temperature fluctuations, polluted water, or swirling dust.

In short, the biggest environmental challenges involve multiple actors and overlapping layers of problems. In 1996 the President's Council on Sustainable Development found that

> conflicts over natural resources increasingly are exceeding the capacity of institutions, processes, and mechanisms to resolve them. Adversarial administrative, legal, and political processes . . . typically stress points of conflict, dividing communities and neighbors. What is usually missing from the process is a mechanism to enable the many stakeholders to work together to identify common goals, values, and areas of interest through vigorous and open public discussion. (PCSD 1997)

Effective and lasting solutions, then, require overcoming significant barriers, such as perspectives that are at odds with one another and incomplete knowledge about the problem. For all the stakeholders involved, any steps toward overcoming these barriers, and working toward a sustainable solution, usually include identifying the source of the conflict. This important task is not always easy to accomplish, as demonstrated below in the discussion of MTM and the conflict that surrounds it.

Mountaintop Mining and Its Impacts

Consider the subject of this book, the regional issue of current national and international import: mountaintop coal mining. The environmental considerations are apparent whether one has any particular environmental expertise or not: enormous chunks of mountains are blasted into rubble, mountain streams filled, waste piled up or impounded in ponds, coal removed, and vast landscapes permanently altered despite reclamation efforts.

What has this done in a matter of a few decades? In a roughly twelve-million-acre region of the Central Appalachian Coal Basin—which incorporates eastern Kentucky, southern West Virginia, southwestern Virginia, and eastern Tennessee—over four hundred thousand acres have been affected by mountaintop mining and valley fill construction (EPA 2012). MTM has torn apart enormous landscapes across those four states, destroying land and altering the flow of many hundreds of streams. The US Environmental Protection Agency reports streams that are completely covered up, and an increase of minerals, such as zinc, sodium, and selenium, and contaminants, such as sulfate, that can harm fish and other aquatic life. These conditions in turn lead to less diverse and more pollutant-tolerant species, forests becoming fragmented and less accommodating to birds and animals, and compacted soils that slow plant growth (EPA 2012).

Along with these changes in the landscape, MTM has divided families, communities, organizations, and municipalities. Even as industry leaders and some government officials in the region in which MTM is practiced defend it as the only viable opportunity for employment, the number of miners has declined sharply during the same time that MTM has expanded (Burns 2007). Sophisticated but expensive mining equipment has become cost effective for mining companies due to the enormous scale on which MTM is practiced. Indeed, according to many, the determination to sustain an economy driven by the coal industry, and specifically by MTM, has kept this large area of the country from developing a more diverse and resilient economy that would also be friendlier to people and the environment (see, e.g., Eller 2008; Flaccavento 2010).

Why would anyone ever allow a practice that is so harmful? Because MTM has had other impacts, too. By providing abundant amounts of coal, it has kept energy prices relatively low for many millions of people. It has provided employment in high-unemployment areas and tax revenues (albeit minimal) to pay for limited social services in those areas. It has rewarded investors in the companies that mine coal as well as utility companies that use it for producing energy and the bankers who finance that mining. Some might think that these benefits cannot possibly outweigh the harm being done. Perhaps, but consider where your electric power comes from at your home or workplace or school, or how your college's endowment or your retirement funds are invested: can you say that you do not benefit from coal mining?[1]

MTM also lays bare, in stark terms, choices that societies face all over the globe. And MTM has had an enormous impact on the lifestyles of stakeholders in the Appalachian region, not only through altering the landscape around them but also by intensifying the conflicts that coal mining historically has engendered.

A Brief History of Appalachian Coal Mining

Residents in the Appalachian coalfields of West Virginia, Kentucky, Virginia, and Tennessee share many cultural and economic connections. Among them are ones that residents in many other regions would recognize: a love of the natural beauty that surrounds them and a shared heritage dating back many generations. As Appalachians, they also share a pride in their independence and resilience in the face of disaster and the challenges of daily life under often difficult circumstances.

Coal is central to the history these residents share, and it bears responsibility for much of their culture, including many of the challenges in their lives. Beginning in the late eighteenth century, residents mined and used coal in small quantities in their homes. In the century that followed, the growing demand for coal to fuel industrial growth led to underground mining on an industrial scale. The history of coal mining in southern Appalachia is one of great economic expansion, especially after railroads were built to carry coal from mine sites to the ports and population centers of the eastern United States.[2] The extraction of coal created a distinction and separation between the remote geographic area that provided the fuel and the places where it was used to forge steel, run factories and trains, and heat the homes of an increasing number of urban dwellers.[3] The effects of that separation remain evident over a century later.

Residents were also separated (both legally and physically) from the land they called home. As it became evident to speculators that the mountains of Appalachia might contain significant amounts of coal, individuals and corporations sought to control the mineral rights of vast areas of mountainous terrain. Complex broad-form deeds were used to acquire those rights from residents, who might not have fully understood what they agreed to. The compensation likely helped some families economically, and concerns they might have were appeased by the guarantee that they would hold "use rights" to their land. Many residents who signed away mineral rights, and some who insisted that they were deceived by company agents, had little idea of the severity of the consequences when the absentee landlords came to set up a mining operation. People who had farmed for generations found their land no longer accessible or usable (Eller 2008; Gaventa 1980; House and Howard 2009).

In the industrial era, coal production was labor intensive, and companies needed more workers at the Appalachian mines than resided in the area. Immigrants from Europe, African Americans from the South, and whites from Appalachia and beyond were among those who worked as miners in the late nineteenth and early twentieth centuries. Rapid growth of the ultracompetitive mining industry brought prosperity for some, especially entrepreneurial coal barons, and the ill effects of mining for many, especially laborers in and around underground mines. Bad health, poisoned water, and isolation are only a few of the trials that families faced in the coalfields. Life in the coal camps built near the mines was often harsh, even as some coal operators provided solid houses for workers and public buildings that anchored lively communities (Shifflett 1991; Tams 2001; Vuranch n.d.).

In many ways the phrase "Coal is King" characterizes the position of the industry in the economy of much of southern Appalachia. However, to stay profitable, the coal industry has had to change in response to developments well beyond the mines. For instance, by the middle of the twentieth century, the railroads, factories, and consumers that once depended almost exclusively on coal for fuel switched to other energy sources, such as diesel, fuel oil, and natural gas. At roughly the same time, technological advances offered the possibility of increased mechanization of underground mining. As companies began to rely on new equipment, workers experienced the destabilizing effects of layoffs and expulsion from company towns (see, e.g., Eller 1982). By the thousands workers were forced to leave the coalfields to seek their livelihood elsewhere (see, e.g., Lewis 1998; Shifflett 1991; Thomas 1998). As another influence on levels of coal production, fluctuations in demand for the soft coal found in Appalachia spurred labor migration in and out of the region and wrenching economic ups and downs for the coal industry (for statistics on coal production, see EIA 2012).[4]

Whether miners used a pickaxe or a continuous-mining machine to gather the mineral deep underground, and whether they put it on a donkey, a railcar, or a conveyor belt to be hauled to the surface, underground coal mining has always been a very dangerous job. The work is physically demanding and the conditions treacherous. If a mine is not properly ventilated, miners can succumb to poisonous gas or spontaneous combustion, and roof cave-ins have killed, injured, and trapped many. Over the years safety has improved through stricter regulation and better technology; however, mine disasters still occur all too frequently.

In the early part of the twentieth century, the threat of injury or worse at work was compounded by the violence of labor relations (see, e.g., Caudill 1963; Gaventa 1980). To keep their workers under their control, mine owners fought unionization, and workers and their families were killed and displaced in labor actions across Appalachia (Fagge 1996). The feature film *Matewan* depicts a violent confrontation in a company town that took place during the West Virginia Coal Wars of 1920 and 1921 (Sayles 1987). The Battle of Blair Mountain is the most famous example of a struggle during the coal wars (Biggers 2006; Shogan 2004; see box on the Battle of Blair Mountain). It was a time of great tension between the coal mine operators and the workers, who were being heavily recruited to join the nascent United Mine Workers of America (UMWA) and other unions. As Harry Caudill puts it, "Nonviolence might never have organized the coalfield. . . . The new Winchester rifles and .38-caliber pistols which appeared in the hands of miners could scarcely have been bought by penniless laborers with little or no credit outside the company commissaries" (Caudill 1963, 198).[5] Unionization took hold for good after the New Deal economic policies and the sweep of labor reforms that President Franklin Roosevelt's administration instituted in the 1930s (Thomas 1998). Union membership reached its peak in the middle of the twentieth century but has declined steadily since then. Some owners and operators continue to fight against unions, and some miners have complained about the corrupt practices of both company owners and union officials (Biggers 2006).

The Battle of Blair Mountain

In Logan County, in far southwestern West Virginia, stands Blair Mountain. Around it swirls a history of battles with coal production at the center. From the perspective of labor history, Blair Mountain was the site of the most important battle of the mine wars of the early twentieth century. On one side were miners seeking to join the United Mine Workers union, and on the other side were coal companies vowing to keep production costs low. In 1921, following months of sporadic violence initiated by company agents, this standoff came to a head when ten thousand miners marched to Blair Mountain to take a stand for organizing as laborers. Several thousand armed police and company security personnel confronted the miners, who wore red bandanas around their necks to show their union solidarity. The fighting was fierce at times; the number of casualties is still disputed, but likely hundreds were killed and wounded. The fighting was halted only after the federal government sent in troops with orders to protect company interests. The Battle of Blair Mountain remains the largest organized labor uprising in the United States.

Two coal companies—Arch Coal and Alpha Natural Resource (formerly Massey Energy)—hold permits to mine Blair Mountain, including areas that were key battlefields during the uprising. After many years of lawsuits brought by environmentalists and historic preservationists, areas of Blair Mountain were designated in 2009 to be included on the National Register of Historic Places, an act that advocates hoped would make mining less likely. Yet those hopes were dashed several months later when a West Virginia state official rescinded the historic designation with the hope of encouraging mining. Legal challenges and protests continued. In June 2011 more than five hundred activists seeking to stop MTM on Blair Mountain re-created the fifty-mile march of 1921. Sporting red bandanas similar to those worn by the original strikers, marchers headed toward Blair Mountain to raise awareness about the history of the area, the dangers of MTM, and the need for a new approach to the region's economy. Along the way they were jeered by some local residents and miners, yet they were also praised and supported more often than they had expected. The march gained national media attention through a CNN special report (see chapter 6).

The Appalachian region experienced classic early "carbon democracy," as described by Timothy Mitchell, a phrase that denotes how the concentration and exploitation of carbon-based resources shape the forms of democracy that result (Mitchell 2009).[6] Coal's exploitation provided people the cheap energy that allowed them to live in concentrated urban centers across the United States, but it also set up tensions between laborers and owners in local settings where mining occurs. Political systems evolved to prop up the sometimes profitable coal industry by supporting owners and by using policing and regulation to keep laborers in line and available when needed.[7] West Virginia, eastern Kentucky, and southwestern Virginia are still largely coal-dependent economies, and the operation of their political systems reflects that economic and political history.[8] One effect has been that residents with complaints against the coal industry have found politicians to be dismissive of their concerns, if not outright hostile in their support of the coal economy.

The scope of coal's economic impact and, perhaps, the power of coal interests have both diminished in recent decades. Despite the value of coal, the riches it has brought to investors, and the wages it eventually offered to unionized workers, the region's populations remain among the poorest people in the nation (McIlmoil and Hansen 2010). In the last half of the twentieth century and the beginning decades of the twenty-first, many underground mines have closed. Unemployment in the coalfields is high. Well over one hundred thousand miners worked in West Virginia in the middle of the last century (O'Leary and Boettner 2011); as of April 2012, they number only about 23,300 (Ward 2012b). Their jobs have been lost through mechanization, changes in the demand for energy, the growth of mining in the western United States and other regions (see Goodell 2006), and the rise of surface mining, as discussed below.

The Practice of Mountaintop Mining

Coalfields residents also share a resilience borne of their boom-and-bust history. But in the latest chapter of that history these residents are deeply divided over MTM. In an effort to extract more coal more cheaply than underground mining methods allow, coal companies have been shifting to surface mining since the 1970s. In contrast to tunneling deep into the mountain, surface mining uses a variety of procedures for removing soil, rock, trees, and other vegetation (called overburden by the mining industry) from the side or top of a mountain to reach the coal seams below the surface. One type of surface mining, called contour mining, takes away part of the side of a mountain, removes the coal, and then replaces the mountain to approximate its original shape.[9]

Mountaintop mining came into being when technological advancements and legal and regulatory interpretations made it possible to mine coal by removing large amounts of overburden (mountaintops) to expose the narrow coal seams lying beneath the overburden. In mountaintop mining, the overburden on the very top of a mountain is blasted with dynamite, then bulldozed into adjacent valleys (EPA 2012; Reece 2006). Layer by layer, successive coal seams are exposed so that the coal can be pulled out with a vehicle called a dragline, which is so enormous that it has to be brought up the mountain in pieces and assembled on site. After the coal is trucked down the mountain to a coal-processing plant, some of the blasted rock and soil is then piled on the original site to build back the now significantly lower mountain. After more than two decades of this practice, a huge amount of rubble that has not been returned to the ridge or mountaintop remains in the valleys and streams of the coalfields. These "valley fills" are the largest man-made structures in the region. And where mountains used to stand, what remains are flattened gray expanses, planted with fast-growing but typically nonnative species of grass.

The acres mined using MTM increased exponentially in the 1990s. Advocates for MTM claim that its practice has reduced energy prices, provided corporate income for shareholders, and secured jobs in high-unemployment areas. They argue that nothing else in the coalfields regions can bring in the tax income needed to pay for schoolteachers and nursing clinics. And, as many of the bumper stickers and license plates on cars plying Appalachian roads read, Coal Keeps the Lights On. Indeed, in 2010 coal generated almost half the electricity used in America (EIA 2012), although that had dropped to just over a third at the time of this book's writing (EIA 2013). At the same time, MTM has torn apart landscapes, altering land and streams on unprecedented scales. Opponents of

FIGURE 2.1. A Red River Coal Company mountaintop mining site in Norton, Virginia. *E. Franklin Dukes.*

MTM argue that the practice buries streams illegally and poisons Appalachia's waters (see fig. 2.1).

Opponents of MTM also complain that massive coal slurry impoundments loom high over schools and homes. These structures hold back millions of gallons of the dark liquid by-product left after coal is sorted and cleaned in preparation for shipping. If the dam holding back one of these impoundments were to burst, as happened most infamously in the Buffalo Creek flooding that killed 125 people, residents would have only seconds to scramble up the mountain to escape a smothering wall of filthy water, sludge, and debris (Stern 2008). A huge slurry spill in Inez, Kentucky, in 2000 confirms that the threat of such incidents is very real (Morrone and Buckley 2011). The intense explosions at MTM sites shatter nerves and weaken house foundations, and the resultant clouds of black dust find their way into every corner of nearby homes. The coal trucks that barrel along the winding roads through the valleys (called hollows, but locally pronounced "hollers") leave behind potholes, accidents, dust, and fearful motorists.

The Pushback against Mountaintop Mining

Complaints about mountaintop mining are not new; the practice—indeed, all surface mining—was controversial from its start. In 1939, decades before MTM evolved, West Virginia was the first state to pass a strip-mining control act (Burns 2007). Ken Hechler, Jay Rockefeller, and other politicians from the region spoke out against surface mining as companies engaged in the practice in earnest, beginning in the 1960s. Struggles over the impacts of surface mining led to the passage of the Surface Mining Control and Reclamation Act of 1977 (SMCRA). The act was designed to hold mining companies responsible for restoring mine sites by bringing surface mining under tighter federal and state regulation. Yet the bill was much weaker than activists had hoped and more in line with demands from industry and labor unions (Montrie 2003, 2011). Through SMCRA, the Office of Surface Mining, Reclamation, and Enforcement was created in the Department of the Interior.

The SMCRA also included provisions that, in hindsight, seem contradictory. It has the dubious distinction of being the first statute to grant legitimacy to the practice of MTM. At the same time, it offered multiple avenues (e.g., lawsuits, public-comment periods) for citizens to express their concerns about mining's environmental consequences (McGinley 2004). When the first MTM projects began blasting away mountaintops, not long after SMCRA's passage, residents near those remote areas complained to local and state regulators and to environmental groups. Getting anyone's attention was difficult at first, but the persistence of lawyers, such as Joe Lovett, and frustrated residents, such as Cindy Bragg, led to the growth of efforts to contest MTM (Loeb 2007; Shnayerson 2008).

Early complaints against MTM focused not only on potential violations of SMCRA but also on the National Environmental Policy Act, which mandates environmental impact studies for projects that use federal funds, and the Clean Water Act, which came into effect in 1972. Much of the fight over whether and how coal companies are granted permits to conduct mountaintop mining on particular sites involves differing interpretations of the Clean Water Act (for further discussion, see chapter 6).

Residents and concerned parties have protested against many aspects of MTM, in addition to the breaches of federal regulations mentioned above. These include

- the damage caused by overloaded coal trucks traveling along narrow roads and one-lane bridges

- the levels of dust near mines and coal preparation plants

- water pollution from run-off near mine sites and filled-in streams

- the labor and business practices of coal operators who frequently declare bankruptcy in order to avoid complying with regulations or paying fines

- inadequate or nonexistent efforts to restore postmining habitat

- the damage done to the landscape in general

All these have been the subject of legal action. Several regional environmental organizations have been prominent plaintiffs in these cases, including the Ohio Valley Environmental Coalition and Kentuckians for the Commonwealth.

Coal companies have fought back and even countersued in order to continue operating. A few companies made it a point to defend against every single challenge (Shnayerson 2008). As a result of this strategy, legal cases began to clog the courts in the early 2000s. This litigation tended to wear down the citizens and groups whose ability to litigate lagged behind that of the better-funded companies. The lengthy appeals process also means that the law is rarely an efficient arbiter. Of even greater concern is that the legal process is not above the influence of politics. In one notorious example, a West Virginia appeals court judge who ruled against Massey Energy, at the time one of the biggest coal companies in the nation, found himself the target of that company's wrath. Massey's CEO, Don Blankenship, retaliated by bankrolling the judge's opponent in the next election.[10]

Litigation has led to changes in the practice of MTM. For instance, the plants where coal is readied for shipping, called prep plants, must ensure that coal dust is contained as much as possible during coal processing. The boundaries of some mining projects have been altered to ensure areas of "setback" intended to protect streams or communities. But legal cases wind their way slowly through courts and often result in equivocal findings. Almost anyone turning to the legal system to get a clear answer as to whether any particular aspect of MTM can be construed as legal was bound to end up disappointed.

Residents, advocacy organizations, and other concerned parties have also taken action outside the courts by lobbying for changes in federal regulations, picketing and demonstrating, and challenging state agencies responsible for administering mining and water law (House and Howard 2009). A community's battle to move an elementary school from beneath the shadow of a coal slurry impoundment included litigation as well as many forms of political lobbying and direct action. In a few instances, parties have also used mediation to address concerns arising out of MTM and other forms of mining (see chapter 4).

The Saga of Marsh Fork Elementary School

Marsh Fork Elementary School, a conventional building set back from the traffic of coal trucks and local residents on the southern end of Coal River Road, was at the center of a firestorm of conflict for over a decade. At issue was the school's location in the midst of active coal production. Just behind the school stands a 385-foot-tall earthen dam that holds back 2.8 billion gallons of the waste left behind after coal processing. Also nearby, a coal preparation plant cleans and processes coal before loading it into railcars for transport.

Ed Wiley, a former coal industry employee who lives near Marsh Fork, first raised the alarm that students at Marsh Fork Elementary were becoming ill from the chemicals and coal dust at the preparation plant. He had figured this out when his granddaughter Kayla and other Marsh Fork students complained of feeling sick while at school. Other concerns related to nearby coal production were also emerging: periodically the school's water became contaminated, and students and their parents feared that the coal waste might break through the dam. While opinions differed as to the dam's strength, everyone had to admit that a breach could result in a catastrophe, especially for the students at Marsh Fork.

Some residents and organizations, such as Ohio Valley Environmental Coalition and Coal River Mountain Watch, offered their support to Ed. When lawyers, such as Joe Lovett, investigated the Massey Energy facilities, they found violations; for instance, coal was being processed closer to the school than was allowable. For its part, Massey Energy insisted that the children were in no danger.

As the explosions at nearby mining sites increased, local residents came to believe that the dam holding back the slurry pond was becoming more vulnerable to collapse, and they determined that protecting the children would

Compounding the tedium and length of the adversarial processes over MTM are technical and scientific uncertainties. Restoration of a blasted mountain to its original conditions is physically impossible, and there is disagreement about whether even a bare functional restoration of streams and the landscape is possible, with a prominent scientific study claiming that efforts at restoration have not been successful (Palmer et al. 2010). A 2011 EPA report asserts that there is little evidence that restoration projects replace aquatic habitat or lost biodiversity (EPA 2011a).

Proponents of MTM have questioned the science used to draw negative conclusions about MTM's impact. Even measuring the impact of mining on a nearby stream is no simple matter. Should the test measure

---

mean moving the school itself. Many activist stakeholders took up the issue of relocating Marsh Fork Elementary School, including Judy Bonds, Lynn Evans, Larry Gibson, Maria Gunnoe, Vernon Haltom, Debbie Jarrell, and Bo Webb. They undertook many direct actions, such as sitting in at the office of West Virginia's governor and at the coal plant and school. State and local officials offered little encouragement or assistance.

After trying to raise awareness about the school in a variety of ways, and to raise money for its relocation, Ed Wiley decided to take his fight to Washington, DC. In August 2006, Ed left Charleston, West Virginia, on foot carrying a huge flag and walked over 450 miles to the nation's capital to tell politicians that the school needed their support. Along the way people cheered Ed on and donated to the fund. In a rousing speech to supporters gathered in Washington, Bo Webb of the local citizens' group called Coal River Mountain Watch proclaimed, "If we fail here as parents, we have failed as Americans."

The vulnerability of the school and the children touched many people. Some of those drawn in by the issue might not have thought of themselves as stakeholders. This was the case for the directors of the Annenberg Foundation, whose donation of $2.5 million in 2010 made it more likely that a new school would be built. The donation was conditional on substantial support from the Raleigh County school board, the School Building Authority of West Virginia, both of which had been rather slow to offer support, and Massey Energy (Buckley and Allen 2011). Funds for the school were supplemented by donations from many individuals and organizations, including Pennies of Promise and Coal River Mountain Watch. The new school opened in early 2013.

the salinity of the water or its conductivity? Should it be measured after a rainstorm or during a dry period? Federal and state regulators, anti-MTM advocates, and coal companies alike have been known to manipulate the tests and results to support their various perspectives. The EPA's insistence on using science advisory boards, which are independent panels of experts, has helped establish scientific measurements for some phenomena. But the bottom line is that agreement over the impact of MTM is elusive.

Another area of uncertainty is the amount of coal left to mine. Coal companies have argued that they will mine coal and employ thousands of miners for the next fifty years or more. Opponents of MTM assert that most of the coal that can be obtained easily and profitably has already been mined and that production will either slow considerably over the next two decades or mining will need to become an even more destructive process to unearth the hard-to-reach coal that remains.

Similarly elusive is any agreement among stakeholders about what should be done about the painful struggle over MTM. Endless legal battles and technical uncertainties have exacerbated the conflict and made it difficult for stakeholders to communicate with one another. As the nation moves toward so-called greener energy—including so-called clean coal or green coal—will MTM have a role? All parties agree that the current situation generates enormous community and political conflict. But they differ bitterly over what might end that conflict.

The irony of the statute known as SMCRA is that while opening the door to MTM, it also established a venue for residents to act against MTM through lawsuits and other actions. Law professor Patrick McGinley asserts, "No other federal environmental regulatory statute contains as many opportunities for citizen involvement nor grants to citizens such a broad array of statutory rights that may be used to influence the law's administration and enforcement than does SMCRA" (McGinley 2004, 48). The legislators who passed SMCRA intended for those affected by mining to be able to voice their concerns and to be part of the regulatory process. Many people have done so, resulting in a fierce fight over MTM. Supporters of MTM believe that without this practice, what they have and value—even if diminished—will disappear entirely. MTM opponents believe that with MTM what they have and value will disappear entirely. When phrased in such stark terms, this conflict appears completely intractable, and it is hard to conclude that anything will change unless and until the coal runs out or economic conditions force a shift away from coal, yet again.

Although some stakeholders are locked in the two-sided battle described above, some points of overlap and agreement are also evident. For one, most stakeholders in the areas affected by MTM share an interest in a strong economy. As in the vision articulated by Sim Ewing in this chapter's opening vignette, stakeholders want productive jobs, a solid tax base, job training for twenty-first-century employment, and opportunities for youth to secure work close to home and for those who have left to seek jobs elsewhere to return. Many of those same stakeholders also want the region to be more livable, with the kinds of services, attractions, and amenities available in other parts of the country.

How can these goals become part of the discussion around MTM? The involvement of a broad range of stakeholders is certainly necessary, yet it might be important to conceive of citizen involvement differently than did those who wrote SMCRA. In chapter 5 we describe a process whereby stakeholders put aside their immediate differences over MTM to talk about a shared future for the region. In effect, they collaborate in an experiment in shared governance. To illustrate what needs to happen to bring about that sort of discussion requires additional attention to the nature of the stakeholders involved and the relationships among them. The next chapter identifies the many stakeholders in the conflict over MTM and explains why it is so deeply difficult for them to collaborate for a shared future while embedded in the conflict. Chapter 3 also begins to look at what can be done to break that impasse.

THREE

Who Is a Stakeholder?

As the newscast described it, actress Daryl Hannah did not resist arrest when she was pulled from the property of Massey Energy, a prominent coal producing company, during a rally and march against mountaintop mining in June 2009. Hannah was not the only celebrity arrested that day on a remote road in southwestern West Virginia. Also arrested were James Hansen, a NASA scientist who had been an outspoken opponent of attempts by government and industry to debunk reports about global warming, and ninety-four-year-old Ken Hechler, a former West Virginia legislator and longtime opponent of surface mining. Arrested along with these well-known figures were other activists, including local residents who believed that coal mining was devastating their region.

The protest route was lined with miners and their families, many of whom loudly jeered as the activists passed by singing "Amazing Grace" as a sign of unity with one another, and as an indication of their wish to communicate with their opponents. Some of the counterprotestors were residents of the area, but, like some of the anti-MTM activists, others had come from elsewhere to take a stand in support of coal mining and the coal industry. Those observers expressed anger and disgust at the protestors and tried to shame them for taking jobs away from Appalachia. Holding signs and banners that denounced those marching as "outsiders" and "tree-huggers," the miners and their families insisted that no one had a right to change the role of coal in their lives. They affirmed their support of the coal industry by chanting "Massey, Massey" as the protestors filed by.

The celebrities and others arrested for blocking traffic on Coal River Road were promptly released; however, the protest action shut down production at the coal-mining site for the whole day. Similar protests continued throughout the summer of 2009, as the conflict over MTM intensified. Over the next year some of the key issues in this long-standing conflict would come to a head. Stakeholders would confront one another in a variety of settings, not only in the coalfields but also outside the region, in law courts, and in the halls of government agencies and Congress in Washington, DC. These activities would involve many stakeholders, well beyond those who had participated in the protest in the summer of 2009.

The preceding vignette depicts the actions of prominent stakehold-ers in the conflict over mining in southern Appalachia during a widely publicized protest. These stakeholders include local residents who oppose new mining permits in their area and activists—some local and some from outside the region—who also oppose MTM entirely. Among the other stakeholders present were active miners; their families; other residents of the region who support mining, including MTM; and officials from the mines and related industries.

The presence of people from outside the region, as well as journalists and onlookers, is a reminder that the broad category of stakeholders can include people who live far from the site where a conflict occurs. In fact, many other key stakeholders might eventually feel the effects of the actions that day in 2009, even if they were neither present at the protest nor aware that it was taking place.

Defining Stakeholders

This chapter introduces readers to the wide range of stakeholders involved in the conflict over MTM and also to the several meanings and uses of the concept *stakeholder* itself. The source of the term is uncer-tain; some say it came into use early in the eighteenth century to refer to someone who holds the stakes in a bet. Another story of its origin refers to the wooden post that marked a section of land claimed by a presumptive owner. In common usage, *stakeholder* has a simple meaning: anyone with an interest to gain or lose in something, such as a conflict, a business venture, or a policy issue. In the conflict field, *stakeholder* is used interchangeably with *parties*, *partisans*, and *disputants*, among other terms, although some scholars and practitioners might distinguish be-tween these.

Stakeholders involved in complex conflicts can be organized into at least three categories:

1. those who will be directly affected economically, physically, emotionally, or socially by an issue (whether they have any ability to effect change concerning the issue or not)

2. those who have a declared interest in the issue but actually might themselves have little directly at stake relative to those in the first category

3. those who have an ability to shape how an issue is articulated and who can prevent or make possible a resolution of that issue

The categories identified above capture three dimensions along which stakeholder roles vary:

1. potential for gain or loss in the conflict

2. degree of interest in the conflict

3. extent of influence in the conflict

In the following sections we use these three dimensions to illuminate the positions of stakeholders and their relationships with one another. Bear in mind that the dynamic nature of conflict means that some stakeholders cannot be placed solely in one category and that an individual's position might shift in response to events in the conflict or the surrounding world.

Before presenting our analysis of stakeholders in the MTM conflict, we must first acknowledge that stakeholders have been categorized in a variety of other ways. The two approaches described below are narrower than ours and are particularly suited to determining how to engage stakeholders in an intervention designed to bring about change in a conflict. For instance, some scholars identify *primary stakeholders* as those who need to be involved in order to achieve a solution and *secondary stakeholders* as those who have an interest of some sort (e.g., something to lose or a commitment to an ideal) but lack the standing to effect change. Designations such as *primary* or *secondary* might convey the impression that certain stakeholders (i.e., primary stakeholders) are intrinsically more important than others, and this concern has led scholars, including us, to avoid these terms.

Another important approach in environmental conflict resolution focuses on how stakeholders frame the conflict (Lewicki, Gray, and Elliott 2003).[1] In the framing approach, stakeholders are not categorized by their positions and interests in the conflict but rather on the basis of the categories or frames they use to understand the conflict and the potential for resolution. One study from this perspective groups stakeholders according to whether they frame the conflict issues "negatively" or "positively" and, more specifically, what attitudes they hold with respect to collaboration, social hierarchy, and power. By taking a framing approach, a third party interested in altering the course of the conflict can bring together those stakeholders who might be most likely to compromise or to otherwise effect change.

A related but simpler set of categories divides stakeholders in a conflict into "moderates, hardliners, external supporters, conflict profiteers, and spoilers" (Burgess 2004). In sum, there are multiple ways to identify and group stakeholders when analyzing a conflict and pursuing its resolution.

POTENTIAL FOR GAIN OR LOSS

When used in the context of an ongoing conflict, the term *stakeholders* often describes the groups or individuals who will feel the effect of the outcome of the conflict or the process of resolution (Burgess 2004; Spangler 2003). From this perspective the most important question is, Does a stakeholder stand to gain or lose anything if the conflict continues, escalates, or is resolved?

In the conflict over issuing new permits for MTM in Appalachia, the stakeholders who would stand to lose or gain most directly include some of the people present at the protest described at the outset of this chapter. For instance, residents of the areas near the mines would certainly feel the impact if mining continues or is prohibited in some way. Those who live close to the mines suffer some of the worst environmental effects of the mining, including effects on health that have only become documented in the last decade or so. Residents report other impacts, too, such as threats from coal trucks barreling along narrow, fragile roads and fear of landslides, mudslides, and sludge dams breaking apart. Property values have plummeted in the areas near mining sites.

One resident-turned-activist, Judy Bonds, had long fought against MTM and its expansion because of the many potential negative effects on local communities, such as dust from coal, frequent flooding, and pollution suspected of causing disease—including, she believed, the cancer that ultimately killed her. Expansion of a surface mine near the small community in the shadow of Coal River Mountain, where she had grown up, forced all her neighbors to sell their property and relocate. Judy held out for years but eventually became unable to stay in her home (Burns 2007). Like Judy, some protestors wanted to be sure that what happened to them as a result of mining would not happen to other communities. Those marching on that June day in 2009 were focused on stopping the Army Corps of Engineers from issuing new mining permits in the area of Coal River Mountain.

Some proportion of residents benefit from the jobs provided through the mining industry. Coal miners and their families are stakeholders by virtue of their occupation and the fact that many economic endeavors in the area are tied to coal mining, such as coal processing and transport. Many miners who showed up to oppose the protest believed that limits on new permits for MTM or on mining in general would directly affect their employment and the welfare of their family members and community. Such a drastic change is a scary prospect for miners, as many jobs had already been forfeited in the move from underground mining to MTM and from Appalachian coalfields to those in the western United States, and unemployment generally is high in the Appalachian coalfields.[2]

Adding to the concern over the decline in employment was the uncertainty caused by all the lawsuits and conflicts over the legality of surface mining, especially MTM. How long would it be possible to continue working as a miner and to live and prosper in the region? Ernest Ruff, from a West Virginia mining family, worries that failing to support coal will leave everyone "sitting in the dark," with no source of fuel for electricity (Werschkul 2010).

For many coalfields residents, mining is more than just a job. It is a way of connecting with their past, with their family, and—for the miners themselves—even with their gender identity as the family provider who works at a hard and dangerous job that benefits the community and nation. For some coalfields residents, multiple generations of men and women in their family have pursued coal mining, and the occupation is, in their words, "in their blood." Many local residents opposed to MTM could make a similar claim that protecting the mountains, perhaps in a long-standing family home, is central to their way of life. For them, MTM threatens their way of life, one that generations have enjoyed. This deep and historic identification with a lifestyle, common to stakeholders on all sides, and the consequences for the MTM conflict are discussed later in this chapter.

The description of the protest that began this chapter and this initial analysis depicts those who stand to lose or gain as two distinct sides, an "us-versus-them" situation (Wondolleck, Gray, and Bryan 2003). The vehicles that shape conflict, such as protest, law, and policymaking, force people into opposing categories. But people on each "side" can hold a variety of perspectives on key aspects of the conflict. Stakeholder groups can comprise people with widely varying views, interests, positions, or behaviors, even though they might come together on particular issues related to the conflict.

For instance, some coalfields residents, including miners, support underground coal mining but are concerned about MTM; some activists, in contrast, oppose all forms of mining but also condemn actions that violate the law, such as occupying coal company property or shutting down production. People in these categories would probably not have attended the protest, although the conflict's impact on them might be great. Understanding a conflict requires attention to the differences among people otherwise grouped together on the basis of their shared relation to gain or loss.

Coal companies and the coal industry are also significant stakeholders, as they stand to gain or lose a lot in the conflict over MTM. Companies themselves comprise a mix of stakeholders, including workers, management, boards of directors, and institutional and individual stockholders; other stakeholders include contractors and suppliers as well as institutional customers such as large utilities. Any efforts to limit the means of producing coal, or to impose stricter regulations, directly affect their business model, profit margin, and the industry's stability.

Many coal companies have operated in the area for decades, and their names—Massey Energy (bought by Alpha Natural Resources in 2011), Arch Coal, Patriot Coal (which filed for Chapter 11 bankruptcy in July 2012), and Consol Energy—are well known in the region. Other companies are relatively new and even less economically stable. Coal companies have always been a mixture of owners from outside the area and those born and raised in Appalachia, such as Don Blankenship, the CEO of Massey Energy at the time of the 2009 protest.

The coal industry clearly benefits directly from the ability to make choices regarding mining and to be free of regulations that impinge on the capacity of companies to mine coal faster and cheaper. Other industries also have a stake in the conflict over MTM. Appalachian mining provides the fuel for many other activities in the region and beyond; however, its role in fueling regional power companies makes Dominion Virginia Power, Consolidated Edison, Allegheny Energy Supply, and Duke Energy substantial stakeholders in the conflict over whether MTM should continue. If permits to mine using MTM are denied, as opponents demand, then power companies might not be able to provide service to customers at the current rates. Even compliance with stricter regulations might mean changes in the economics of coal-fired power plants. Concerns over coal production, combined with the pressure to limit carbon emissions and to take advantage of falling prices for natural gas, have led some power companies to switch to cleaner-burning fuels (Raz and Silverman 2011).

No doubt the next point is obvious: the people who receive their power from coal-fired power plants could also possibly gain or lose depending on the outcome of the MTM conflict. Coal from Appalachia powers homes and businesses in many areas. Most of the residents who benefit quite directly from the coal industry are unaware of their connection to the conflict over mining, and more than a few would be concerned to learn that its outcome could mean higher electric bills or a switch to how the power they receive is produced.[3]

People who live farther from the mining sites can also be affected by the environmental impact of MTM and thus are stakeholders in the conflict. To the extent that mining degrades the water quality and buries streams that are essential to maintaining a watershed, then many people in the major river valleys of the eastern half of the United States, such as the Ohio River valley, are affected by diminished water quality and soil contamination and erosion. Many conflict practitioners who work on environmental issues take a "watershed approach," which traces the effects downstream from the source of pollution. A watershed approach uses the actual hydrology of an area to determine who the stakeholders are and how their interests might be configured. In a conflict over the kind of water pollution that is often produced through mining, for instance, those parties upstream from the polluted water might have a very different set of interests than those situated downstream, where the environmental impact is felt. Those upstream might even be considered contributors to the conflict through their activities as farmers, miners, industry owners, or users of the water.

Brad Kreps and the Clinch-Powell Clean Rivers Initiative

One of the major stakeholder groups in Appalachia's southwestern Virginia is the international conservation organization The Nature Conservancy (TNC). TNC's local office is in Abingdon, Virginia, a town enriched by coal money but lying just outside the coalfields.

TNC's focus in the region is the Clinch River. The Clinch has nineteen rare fish species and twenty-eight rare mussels and is considered "our nation's most important river for imperiled freshwater animals," according to TNC. As is true with other such rivers that support rare freshwater mussels, there have been declines in the health of mussel populations along significant stretches of the Clinch. These declines have prompted action from TNC and other environmental advocates.

Brad Kreps directs the TNC's Clinch Valley Program. In 2004 he completed a yearlong program, the Virginia Natural Resources Leadership Institute, that offered extensive training in consensus building among diverse and often conflicting environmental interests. Shortly after that experience he began to strategize about ways of engaging industry and regulators in considering the impacts of coal mining and other activities on the Clinch River and its tributaries.

Kreps took on an ambitious task: rather than attack the companies for the environmental impacts of mining, he sought to engage companies in a collaboration to understand scientifically what was harming the Clinch. In a region where it is common to see only two sides—pro-coal and pro-environment—Kreps and his colleagues ventured beyond those caricatures.

For this sensitive subject, the Conservancy and a steering committee of balanced interests decided that an open symposium that would include field trips and presentations focused on science and knowledge would be the best way to begin the process of engagement. In 2007 the symposium Kreps and others planned brought together university researchers, coal-mining companies, federal and state agencies, and private organizations with the goal of creating a "framework for establishing, funding, and sustaining an organized effort to advance critical scientific research in these globally significant watersheds" (CPCRI 2007).

This symposium had its intended effect. It led to the formation of an ad hoc group, the Clinch-Powell Clean Rivers Initiative, with diverse leadership and participation. A 2010 follow-up symposium and periodic meetings of the initiative follow this mission: "The Clinch-Powell Clean Rivers Initiative is an ambitious two-state river coalition that works to protect and restore water quality in North America's most important river for rare and imperiled freshwater animals. We are a diverse group of agencies, research scientists, conservation organizations, and industry leaders" (CPCRI 2010).

The last sentence is an understatement. This coalition of environmentalists, coal companies, and agencies is very rare. It is an extraordinary achievement for Kreps and his partners and collaborators. Besides his leadership in this science-based effort, he is an active participant in the Clinch River Valley Initiative, profiled in chapter 5.

Those who live more remotely from a site where environmental damage might occur are often considered to have less at stake, and their involvement is linked to their "interest" in the conflict, as described in the next section. But this proposition is contestable. In a time when the general effects of climate change are of concern, any activity that is viewed as contributing to global warming attracts the attention of people well beyond the immediate context. The deforestation associated with MTM, as well as the impact of burning coal and other fossil fuels, have heightened the concern of many stakeholders who live far from the Appalachian region and have mobilized them to become involved. Some assert that their stake in the conflict is just as important as that of people who live closer or depend on coal for a living.

This perspective is articulated by a group called Interfaith Power and Light. Based outside the coalfields region, they nonetheless assert they have something to lose in the fight over MTM.

> As communities of faith organizing a religious response to global warming, we believe that climate disruption is among the greatest challenges that humanity has ever encountered. We commit ourselves to the moral imperative of preserving and protecting the planet for generations to come. There can be no effective strategy to address climate disruption without significant restructuring of our electricity production, including a rapid and just transition from antiquated coal power generation. . . . We know that all forms of coal mining are dangerous, imperil human health, and degrade landscapes and human communities. Particularly egregious is mountaintop removal mining. . . . We therefore oppose mountaintop removal mining and advocate for its immediate discontinuation. (IPL n.d.)

LEVEL OF INTEREST

The US Environmental Protection Agency defines *stakeholders* as "individuals or representatives from organizations or interest groups that have a strong interest in the Agency's work and policies" (EPA n.d.). In this definition the term *interest* could be interpreted as applying to parties with a material stake in the conflict or parties who have an interest in the sense of being motivated to engage in it or follow it. Their reasons could be nonmaterial, such as acting on their values.

The people who attended the protest described at the beginning of this chapter were clearly interested in the conflict, and many had something to lose or gain. Evidence of the high degree of interest of some local residents who oppose MTM also comes in the form of the organizations that they have started and joined. The Ohio Valley Environmental Coalition, Coal River Mountain Watch, Kentuckians for the Commonwealth, and Southern Appalachian Mountain Stewards are among the most established of the many groups that help residents and other interested parties channel their concerns into collective action.

To act on their strong interest in the conflict, miners and their supporters might turn first to their unions, or to the state coal associations. A number of newer organizations formed as evidence began accumulating of the harmful effects of valley fill and as EPA indicated that it would conduct a closer review of permits granted to mining enterprises. These groups include Friends of Coal and FACES of Coal (Federation for American Coal, Energy and Security), which represent the interests of those who support all forms of coal mining, including MTM.

Not all the people present at the 2009 protest had a stake in the sense of standing to lose or gain something specific or immediate. Among those who helped organize the anti-MTM activities were members of an organization called (at the time) Mountain Justice Summer (MJS; Shapiro 2010), formed by experienced activists who had worked on environmental actions elsewhere in the country. Many of them became involved in working against MTM because of their deep commitment to protecting the environment.

Beginning in 2004 young people from around the United States joined the MJS encampment each summer. Some group members permanently relocated to a community near Coal River Mountain and thus came to have a direct stake in MTM to match their already strong interest. In contrast, other MJS members would move on after a period of residence near the mines.

Several large environmental advocacy groups have a strong interest in MTM, including the Sierra Club and Earthjustice. In 2002 the

Sierra Club started what has become a large campaign that not only opposes MTM but also works to reduce all forms of coal mining. Called Beyond Coal, the campaign focuses on promoting alternative energy sources (Sierra Club n.d.). Earthjustice has taken a significant interest in the court cases and legislation focused on MTM permitting, protecting water quality, and other issues addressed in the legal arena. These groups articulate and act on values such as protecting the environment, limiting fossil fuel use, developing green energy, and conserving resources.

These groups, and other like-minded groups and individuals, often state that they are involved in controversial issues such as MTM because they are acting in the public interest. Who decides what is in the public interest? Is it even realistic to think that a large and diverse population would have a unitary interest in MTM or any other cause? These questions are difficult, yet government agencies, politicians, and advocacy groups often justify their actions as furthering or protecting the public interest. But what about the notion of the public itself as a stakeholder?

If a conflict is so destructive that it threatens infrastructure or everyday interaction, many people would agree that resolving it is in the public interest. But the general public is largely unaware of many conflicts, and it is often hard to gauge the level of public interest or to determine what actions the public—a highly diverse group—might support in relation to the conflict. As in many environmental conflicts, the real difficulty that the conflicting parties have is getting the public to take an interest in what they believe to be a just cause.

Journalists and media outlets see their job as, in part, looking out for the public interest. Since the mid-1990s, certain local journalists (e.g., Paul Nyden) and national journalists (e.g., Penny Loeb and Joby Warrick) have covered the conflict over MTM, although most local news media have avoided it. Ken Ward Jr., a journalist with the *Charleston Gazette*, has been the most consistent and persistent journalist addressing MTM and other conflicts over coal (see box on Ken Ward Jr. in chapter 6).

Reaching the public and convincing them of their interest in MTM are goals that drive some of the journalists engaged in the conflict. For example, Antrim Caskey, a photojournalist with little direct connection to the region, chose to relocate to the Coal River Road area to cover the story. Caskey, who described herself as an "embedded journalist" with Mountain Justice Summer and other anti-MTM groups in southern West Virginia, merged her strong interest in MTM as an environmental issue with her desire to have a physical stake in it as well (Caskey 2010; Goodman 2010).

Increasingly, journalists use both conventional media, such as television and newspapers, and also new forms of electronic and social media, such as blogs, RSS, Twitter, and Facebook, to keep attention focused on whichever issues interest them. Some news outlets take a clear position on the MTM conflict, and for all, maintaining the appearance of journalistic objectivity when writing about it is very challenging.

Some stakeholders have a strong interest in the conflict out of their concern for protecting business and industry from excessive government regulation. Certain industries, investor groups, and pro-business organizations have a high level of interest in working against limits on commercial and industrial development. For instance, the chambers of commerce at the local, state, and national levels generally want government to stay out of those regulatory processes that they believe can best be handled by industry. The chambers also may want state and local regulators, who they argue better understand the issues than do federal regulators, to have more autonomy from national agencies.

In the previous chapter, Sim Ewing expressed an interest in seeing people in his region plan constructively for the future. Although he takes no stand on the future of coal, he is typical of those who comprehend the effect of this conflict on the region's future. It might be possible to understand his involvement in MTM-related issues as emerging from a sense of having a material stake in his region. But his high degree of interest can also be explained through his own personality and values. After all, not everyone who has a material stake in an issue decides to act on it, especially when they face opposition. When stakeholders who have the stature of Sim Ewing become involved in a conflict, they can have significant influence. Ewing's position as a high-level university official has allowed him to engage with some of those stakeholders who have the greatest influence, a dimension of the stake-holder category described below.

LEVEL OF INFLUENCE

Some individuals and groups have more ability than others to shape how an issue is articulated and to prevent or facilitate a resolution of that issue. In the example at the beginning of the chapter, few of those attending the rally and protest had the ability directly to change the course of the conflict, at least not without considerable assistance from more powerful individuals and institutions. Stakeholders with an ability to effect change directly are crucial to any resolution process. Definitions of *stakeholder* written into law and policy can determine who has decision-making authority and thus influence in that sense.

In an environmental conflict, the stakeholders with the greatest influence usually have it because they possess material resources, legal rights, a leadership position, or political power; they are situated to act on the issues involved. For example, the owners of the property or resources slated for mining, the key regulators who make and enforce the rules for granting permits for mine operations, or the financiers of the whole enterprise all have significant influence in the MTM conflict.

The coal industry's degree of influence in the MTM conflict is very high. Mine owners and operators can determine the next steps in the conflict. Organizations that work on behalf of the coal industry, such as the West Virginia Coal Association (WVCA), are also influential. When Bill Raney, the longtime president of the WVCA, represented the industry group in public settings, he had the authority and the legitimacy to speak on behalf of miners, owners, and others. Officials in a wide range of related industries, such as power utilities, also possess some degree of influence.

Unions are designed to increase the influence of laborers beyond what they possess when acting as individuals. Usually this influence is used in negotiations with management over job-related issues, such as wage increases, benefits, and safety procedures, but it can also be relevant to broader conflicts. For the most part the mining unions have supported

MTM, although the support is not without controversy, as mining jobs have decreased considerably through the practice, and some underground miners do not favor it for those and other reasons (Roberts 2008). Unions could be a powerful voice but are often compelled to stand with the industry on MTM and other issues in order to preserve their bargaining power when contract negotiations come around.[4] In mines that are not unionized, such as those owned by the company formerly known as Massey, miners tend to follow their company's preference for or against MTM.

Other significant categories of stakeholders with influence include the public officials whose decision making can change the course of the conflict. As discussed in chapter 1, the federal and state governments regulate surface mining. EPA plays a role in enforcing policies, as does the US Army Corps of Engineers, which is directly involved in approving permits for new mines and valley fills. The state-level environmental protection agencies have been delegated the authority to enforce federal regulations under the Clean Water Act, the Surface Mining Act, and other legislation. This delegated authority is called primacy. To gain and retain this authority the state agencies must demonstrate to the appropriate federal agencies that they are enforcing the federal regulations, a practice that is normally without controversy. But the potential threat of withdrawing state primacy and taking over permitting directly is a tool that the EPA and other federal agencies can and do use to ensure proper oversight of regulations. This threat has shaped actions involving MTM.

State government agency interests are varied, and their roles often controversial. From industry perspectives, sometimes those state regulators are preoccupied with securing fines rather than solving problems. From the perspective of many environmental advocates, state regulators often do the bidding of industry. From the federal agencies' perspective, their state colleagues are sometimes overly solicitous of local economic conditions, a view occasionally reinforced by the revolving door of employment between agency and industry. Finally, regulators from states downstream from MTM activity may be concerned about insufficient protections. For example, Tennessee regulators threatened action against

Virginia regulators for allowing harm to the Clinch River as it entered Tennessee, until Brad Kreps's efforts helped them work together.

Staff at state and federal agencies themselves describe many other challenges:

- Agency leadership may change frequently, as governors and the president appoint the heads of state and federal agencies, and priorities may swing wildly after an election.

- Agencies may find themselves at odds with other agencies at the same level but with competing mandates (e.g., economic development vs. environmental protection).

- Federal and state agencies frequently have histories of strained relationships, outright conflict with one another, and different expectations about their roles.

- Individuals who work for regulators also live in communities and may be conflicted about the hardships that certain decisions may impose.

Other public officials also have influence over the course of the MTM conflict. Elected officials at federal and state levels can vote in ways that favor or constrain MTM. According to the US Institute of Peace, when governments gain much of their income from natural resources, they are susceptible to corruption, and officials are "more likely to take bribes, funnel public funds to private accounts, and ignore environmental degradation, resource-related violence, and human rights violations" (USIP 2007, 7). The charge of being in the pocket of the coal industry has been leveled against many politicians from coal-mining states who take money for their campaigns from coal interests. Nor are judges above suspicion, which takes a different form depending on whether they are elected or appointed. It is notable, however, that most public officials from coal states are very reluctant to criticize the coal industry.

Other community leaders can also influence a conflict. For instance, religious leaders have played significant roles in the MTM conflict (see the box on Dennis Sparks in chapter 4). Religious observance is an important part of life for many living in the region, and a pastor can have significant influence on a congregation. Many churches in the communities near the mines are small, but some are affiliated with regional, state, or national organizations that provide a larger audience. Several Christian denominations have involved large numbers of their members in the MTM conflict, including many living outside the coalfields. Relying on scripture, they have fashioned quite distinct and diverse ways of thinking about the issues. For some, being a good Christian requires conserving God's bounty (i.e., ending MTM); others note that God put coal and other resources on earth for humans to use and thereby prosper.

Celebrities rarely possess the legal standing or political positioning to influence a conflict, yet they can possess significant influence all the same. Their fame and recognition (sometimes adoration) by the public can ensure that their perspective gains attention. In the 2009 protest, the involvement of Daryl Hannah and other notables probably increased the news coverage. Other celebrities have also come to influence the course of the MTM conflict, such as Kathy Mattea and Ashley Judd against MTM, and Hank Williams Jr. and Ted Nugent for coal interests.

Writers such as novelist and columnist Silas House and journalist Michael Shnayerson have brought the conflict to the public's attention (House and Howard 2009; Shnayerson 2008). Robert Kennedy Jr.'s involvement in making and starring in one of the many documentary films about MTM lent the cause additional support and reached a national market (Haney and Rhodes 2011). In some instances, celebrity involvement can play a crucial role in persuading powerful and influential people, such as industry leaders or politicians, to reconsider their position in a conflict. Even as celebrities draw public attention to an issue, their involvement has a downside. Most celebrities have little time to devote to causes. Some longtime activists complain about celebrities who "parachute in" for events and never gain an understanding of people living in the area and working on the conflict on a daily basis. The appearance of a celebrity at an event can even take away from the message other stakeholders hope to communicate. A few celebrities, though, are notable in their commitment to the MTM issue.

Kathy Mattea

> I'm prosperity and poverty,
> I'm a scoundrel and a saint.
> I'm loved, reviled, misunderstood,
> I'm hope in a hopeless place.
>
> —"Hello, My Name Is Coal," lyrics by Larry Cordle and Jenee Fleenor,
> sung by Kathy Mattea on her album *Calling Me Home*

Kathy Mattea may be her own category of stakeholder; certainly she defies the stereotypes and easy caricatures that prominence in MTM issues often brings. She is a celebrity, a Grammy Award–winning country and folksinger who makes headlines when she speaks out against mountaintop mining. But the headlines, and the label as an anti-MTM activist, offer only a superficial view of her deeper interests. She has strong concerns about the impacts of mountaintop mining, both on the mountains and on the people. But she is from West Virginia, the granddaughter of two miners, and in her interviews she is quick to point out that she is not against coal or coal mining.

Although she has been speaking about public issues for nearly two decades—she was one of the first country music stars to speak out about AIDS—she is not entirely comfortable with her role as a spokesperson for those battling MTM. "I'm very scared about this; I'm not very comfortable. . . . I was not born an activist, but I try to live a life with some integrity in it" (House and Howard 2009, 116). In fact, it wasn't until the 2006 Sago mine disaster in West Virginia, where she sang at the funeral for the twelve miners killed, that she found herself deeply involved in mining issues.

Mattea wants to bring the competing sides together. She refuses to demonize the companies or the miners, and she believes that she has a role in finding ways of meeting the needs of all parties. Indeed, the songs she chose to sing on her 2008 album, *Coal*, and the 2012 album, *Coming Home*, demonstrate empathy for the miner's world and the harm of mining. Although proclaiming that she lacks the mediation skills to bring about the conflict's transformation, she is convinced that the solutions lie within the power of the key stakeholders themselves. One can say that MTM is wrong while empathizing with those who are responsible for that wrong.

The Roles of Third-Party Stakeholders

The issues that MTM raises are contested by stakeholders in the news media, the courts, the administrative arena of permit applications and public hearings, and the political world. Less prominent than these highly visible arenas for disputing, but nonetheless significant in the Appalachian communities that experience MTM, are an array of efforts designed to attenuate the harm that such conflict may bring. In some cases, these efforts address underlying issues that the better-known forums cannot. They can shape stakeholders' behavior and may make profound differences in their relationships and interests.

Leading many of these efforts is a less visible category of stakeholders—third parties seeking to change the relationships or the outcomes for the conflicting parties. Names for these roles include *conciliator, mediator,* and *consensus builder.* The common denominator among them is that an individual or organization works to bring together conflicting parties to address dimensions of the conflict. Individuals with a direct stake in the conflict can play this role, but more commonly it involves an outsider with little or no apparent stake in the conflict itself.

As such, these third parties at times channel stakeholders into entirely different types of behavior than they might otherwise display, providing forums where parties to the conflict might shift their interactions (at least temporarily) from protest and reaction to reflection, dialogue, and problem solving. When these forums are successful, they also can help confirm the legitimacy of parties who previously may have lacked credibility or standing. Although the terms *conciliator, mediator,* and *consensus builder* are often used interchangeably, and indeed an individual may take on more than one role, the differences among the roles are worth understanding, because they have different impacts on stakeholders.

CONCILIATORS

Conciliation involves steps taken by a party to reduce hostility, lower tension, correct misperceptions, improve communication, and, at times, create a favorable climate for negotiation. Often a figure of some stature to the disputants uses his or her position to act as a conciliator by beginning and leading the conciliation process. Conciliation also is often associated with religious groups and is a particular focus of Quakers and Mennonites. An example of conciliation by a direct stakeholder in the MTM conflict is the effort by former West Virginia governor Joe Manchin III to bring together stakeholders and issue a highly visible call against violence and for dialogue (see description in chapter 4).

Conciliation encompasses resolution but goes beyond an agreement to attempt to address the relationships among the parties. To reconcile stakeholders is to create a relationship where parties recognize and acknowledge one another's identity and worth. Community reconciliation is a process through which groups of people either in active conflict or who otherwise retain a legacy of harm, grievances, fear, or mistrust from previous events come together to

- Understand the sources of their differences, including initial harms or perceived harms done to or by one another and resultant actions on all sides.

- Establish or restore fractured and often asymmetric relationships such that parties perceive good faith through repair of past or ongoing harms, and reestablish or deepen trust among individuals and groups who previously had little trust for each other.

- Reform systems and institutions that either led to harm or deepened the conflict or issue at hand.[5]

The process of conciliation may occur in a wide variety of situations, which may involve relatively balanced power and shared culpability, requiring parity of actions by all parties consistent with that balance. Or the situations may involve a significant harm that one party has inflicted upon another, where power differences and opportunity for continuing harm favor one party over another and where responsibility and opportunity for action lie primarily with the more powerful party.

MEDIATORS

Mediation is the assistance of an impartial third party (the mediator) in negotiations over a discrete set of issues, typically involving some impasse and a pressing need for agreement. A term more reflective of the actual procedure may be *mediated negotiations*, which appropriately removes the focus from the mediator and places it on the negotiating stakeholders.

Such assistance can take many forms, including procedural and substantive advice, and is sometimes described by other terms, including *facilitation* and *peacebuilding*. Mediation, during which the mediator cannot impose any decision, sometimes is mistaken for *arbitration*, where an arbitrator rules in favor of one of the parties.

Mediation comprises a broad set of procedures. These range from the "muscle mediation" activities of a diplomat or an old-fashioned labor mediator, who often brings pressure to bear on the disputants to reach an agreement, to what is sometimes called transformative mediation. A transformative mediator generally recognizes the impact of the mediation process on parties, relationships, and institutions beyond the immediate issues under dispute and proposes consideration of that impact in the purposes, goals, and evaluation of the mediation process (Bush and Folger 1994).[6] During a mediated negotiation, the mediator helps the disputing parties exchange ideas, promises, threats, or other information related to one or more issues. A distinction is commonly made between *positional negotiation*, which involves little or no analysis of the wants and needs underlying a party's stated positions, and *interest-based negotiation*, which attends to those underlying wants and needs (Fisher and Ury 1983).[7]

A mediator typically conducts a formal or informal situation assessment before convening the mediation. As we describe in chapter 4, the Keystone Center, an organization that facilitates different types of interaction among parties to environmental conflicts, conducted such an assessment for the Coal River watershed, where they found that "prospects for some kind of full consensus about the legitimacy of mountaintop mining from a public policy perspective are remote" (Adler and Thompson 2008, 21). In other words, a mediated negotiation about the future of MTM was not worth investigating further. But the Keystone Center researchers also found more promising options for consensus building on related issues, such as community development and environmental protection.

Consensus builders work with stakeholders to foster broad agreement on changes in policy and practices. Consensus building is explored in depth in chapter 5, which specifically highlights the Clinch River Valley Initiative undertaken in southwestern Virginia by one of us (Frank), his associate Christine Gyovai, and a large group of stakeholders.

The answer to this question is not simple, and it depends on one's perspective on the conflict. But the answer is important, because it sheds light on who is empowered to participate in doing something about the conflict. Identifying three dimensions of stakeholders offers a way of thinking about power dynamics in relation to a conflict. For instance, the stakeholders with the greatest influence in the conflict possess certain forms of authority, and they are often the most important stakeholders to involve when attempting change.

It might seem odd or unfair that someone in a state capital, perhaps hours away from where mining takes place, can have more influence than the people living right in the midst of the action. Regardless of whether this seems appropriate, the reality of complex environmental conflicts is that many times those closest to the environmental impact have the least influence and are the most likely to be ignored in some efforts to bring stakeholders together. For this reason, stakeholders who lack influence might find it difficult to gain recognition from other stakeholders or the public.

Ed Wiley felt this way when industry executives and politicians repeatedly refused to listen to his claims that an elementary school located on Coal River Road was vulnerable to a sludge dam situated directly above it should that dam fail and flood the valley communities below, and that the planned MTM in the area would make the dam even more unstable (Cavanaugh and Wood 2010; Shnayerson 2008). Larry Gibson felt this way as mountaintop mining began to claim land on Kayford Mountain, where his family had lived for generations. His frustrations led him to become an active Keeper of the Mountains, welcoming thousands of people to his family home to witness MTM up close.

In some instances the tables turn and the most influential stakeholders are not those who own the mines or make the political decisions but rather those individuals and groups that can claim a direct and immediate connection to the place where the conflict has most impact. For instance, being an "insider" or "on the ground" or "a local" can be valued highly and hard to dismiss, especially when such stakeholders' claims are brought to a broad audience. Deep-rooted American values that emphasize an individual's

FIGURE 3.1. Keeper of the Mountains Larry Gibson on Kayford Mountain, West Virginia, with students from George Mason University.
Susan F. Hirsch.

right to protect his or her home and livelihood are powerful and, in some instances, can grant coalfields residents a kind of moral authority in the conflict that trumps the influence of those whose authority rests on owner-ship or political office.

Note that an insider's moral authority can be used in advocacy for pro-hibiting MTM or defending it. When the pro-coal activists at the June 2009 rally told "outsiders" to go home, they were drawing on this notion that only those who experience the conflict directly should have a say. A claim to insider status is a way of valuing one's own approach and em-powering oneself over someone who is an outsider or someone who has an interest. The insider-outsider divide is commonly invoked in environmen-tal conflicts, and the pro-environment movement itself often has to deal with the charge that some among its adherents are meddling outsiders.

The example of one stakeholder's moral authority pitted against an-other's political power or material wealth highlights two other key points about stakeholders. First, the stake that someone has in a conflict is often impossible to measure. How can we gauge the emotional pain of losing one's job and having to leave the community to find work elsewhere? Sec-ond, even if the pain of leaving one's community could be measured just as easily as, for instance, the material or economic loss attached to relocation, could it be compared to other experiences, such as chronic illness or the frustration of being unable to act on one's values? Stakeholders' interests are often simply incommensurable: impossible to measure or not comparable in any objective way. As the apples-and-oranges analogy suggests, the interests differ so thoroughly in quality that they cannot be measured against one another—especially when the interests are intangible and reflect values, beliefs, and aspects of identity or culture. Conciliators, mediators, and consensus builders know that they must be sensitive to those situations when stakeholders in conflict are acting on intangible but very real sentiments, but even talking about a conflict is not always easy when claims about lifestyle lie at its core.

When a Way of Life Is at Stake

Some of those participating in the protest and counterprotest depicted at this chapter's outset were fighting hard out of concern that the way of life they (and their ancestors) have known is about to disappear. On the surface it might seem that the conflict over MTM is about technical legal issues, or protecting the natural environment, or preserving jobs, and those indeed are important dimensions of the conflict. But this fight is also about deep personal, historical, and cultural connection to a place (see, e.g., Geller 2009). A "complicated cultural politics" results from the location of this place "both at the heart of the national industrial market economy and within a marginalized mountain rurality" (Scott 2010, 2).

The mountains have hosted distinct ways of living for many centuries. Describing the "ways of life" that Appalachians value presents a challenge, if we want to avoid either romanticizing or denigrating them. People living in the region have been infamously stereotyped and misrepresented. Even identifying residents as "Appalachians" or "coalfields residents" can be directly offensive to some, and the act of having a label imposed on you can feel disempowering. When used in mainstream popular culture, the term *hillbilly* can connote an uneducated, backward, and or even violent person. In contrast to these negative cultural stereotypes, residents themselves would describe their lifestyle quite differently and in far more positive terms, even while admitting to challenges endemic to the region. Local residents tend to emphasize that their way of life includes strong family ties, an ethic of hard work, and religious observance. Some local people even have proudly reclaimed *hillbilly* to reflect those characteristics.

At the same time, many residents acknowledge that their communities have been marginalized politically, economically, and socially. As a result, life has been hard for many families. Compared to other areas of the United States, services in the coalfields of Appalachia—such as education and health care—are well below the norm. Efforts to boost regional development as part of the Great Society program of the 1960s did not succeed in economic growth that benefited most residents (Eller 2008). Yet the ties that bind people to this region of hills and hollows can be very strong, and at their core is an emotional connection to ways of life that are possible only in a mountainous, and thus somewhat historically isolated, environment.

The lifestyle that some residents hope to preserve includes residing in the hollow under a mountain ridge where it is possible to hunt or pick wildflowers or use nearby streams for swimming and fishing. Some families trace their connection back many generations to particular hollows or mountains where forebears farmed, and family graveyards can remain in use for centuries. An enduring connection to particular places in and around the mountains shapes a way of life that includes living remotely from others in a small, close-knit community.

Since the late nineteenth century, the mountains have also provided the main source of income and a distinct lifestyle organized around coal mining. Families who have made a living mining coal share a bond with the mountains and, because the jobs are hard and treacherous, with one another. Being a coal miner fuels a strong sense of identity for men, both young and old, and a much smaller number of women (for a discussion of mining and gender identity, see Scott 2010). Wives, daughters, and other family members of miners have their own experiences of a way of life shaped by hard work and all too frequent tragedy. These difficulties have led some parents to urge their children to seek a life outside the mines and the coalfields.

Although these perspectives may reflect very different experiences, coalfields residents also share a common positive perspective on their surroundings, whatever the job they hold or their stance on MTM. Call it Appalachian culture or southern mountain culture, the way of life associated with the mountains has common themes that are expressed through music, folklore, and dance. Songs that depict life in the mountains range from the country ballads about the bittersweet life of a coal-mining family, to the folk songs that valorize struggles to unionize workers, to the melodious celebration of Appalachia's beauty in John Denver's "Country Roads," to Kathy Mattea's songs on her album *Coal*, as just a few examples.

These sentiments held by mining supporters and local anti-MTM activists are not so different, as each values a way of life that is intimately connected to the mountains. Any threats to that setting—whether through polluting the landscape and water or limiting access to resources—can be threatening to someone's way of life.

Why is this important, beyond the obvious reason that people tend to avoid and fear drastic change? A threat to one's way of life also calls into question one's very identity, one's sense of self. Some commentators have tried to depict residents of Appalachian coalfields as stubbornly unwilling to change or to adopt the more "modern" lifestyles of Americans in other regions. A closer look at the region's history counters that perspective by showing that resistance was often transformative rather than protective of the status quo and by highlighting innovative contributions of residents (see, e.g., Barry 2012; Eller 2008; Gaventa 1980; Hufford 2003; Montrie 2011). Still, when strong identity attachments or cultural understandings are challenged, people find it difficult to face the prospect of change, and they can feel threatened. The rise of MTM has made that threat more compelling by pushing people off their land and out of their communities and posing a challenge to everyone's way of life.

In most cases all three stakeholder dimensions—potential for gain or loss in the conflict, degree of interest in the conflict, and extent of influence in the conflict—are relevant when analyzing a conflict and figuring out how to address it. Over the course of a conflict, the extent to which one or another of these dimensions applies to a particular stakeholder might change. Conflicts develop over time, and a stakeholder's level of interest in a conflict or ability to affect the conflict is subject to many influences. For instance, some stakeholders with very high levels of interest initially can end up burned out, especially if they engage in fighting about the issue for a long time or under difficult circumstances. External events, relationships among group members, and the dynamics of the conflict, including the actions of third parties, can cause a stakeholder to change in all three dimensions.

Despite the deep ties and connections to the mountains, some key decisions about what will happen will come at the hands of people and forces located outside the coalfields. In the next chapters we continue to explore stakeholder dynamics inside and outside the region.

FOUR

Conflict Dynamics and Stakeholder Experiences

On an unseasonably warm day in December 2009, two activists who oppose mountaintop mining speak of their work. Frank and several colleagues, seeking an entry into the conflict, carefully navigate through the opening moves of a conversation, aware of what is perhaps a subliminal caution as the activists probe them for their willingness to listen and hear or, conversely, their potential intention to use their words against them, perhaps to alter their meaning to their disadvantage, to betray that meaning to those who would seek to defeat their cause, or simply to co-opt them in some way. For how many interviews, public meetings, protests, court hearings, and casual conversations must they hold up this same psychic shield?

Due perhaps to earlier positive interactions with one of the activists and an introduction from the cousin of the other, Frank and colleagues are able to move past the opening encounter into deeper issues. The conversation eventually turns toward the question of the activists' personal safety. A number of activists have been threatened by phone or mail, and in person there have been numerous intense confrontations. A notorious example occurred during public hearings on US Army Corps of Engineers' Nationwide 21 permits, when many of those opposing MTM were asked to leave by state police who said that their safety could not be guaranteed.

"We are fine," they protest, "we have no concerns here."

"Really?" they are asked. "Do you take precautions?"

"Well . . . ," and the story unfolds, seemingly as much a revelation to these activists as they tell of their lives as to those listening. There are the usual encounters that anyone involved in controversial issues may expect: nasty letters published in the newspapers, angry comments in blogs and other online forums, hostile interactions at public meetings, neighbors hurling invectives.

But for these activists, there is more: rambling late-night telephone calls from anonymous speakers, sometimes seeming only to desire to vent, other times edging across the line that separates intense opposition from veiled threat. Perhaps a car following them down the isolated country road of their hometown has nothing to do with their work against MTM; perhaps it has everything to do with that work. That noise outside their house may be a deer, or a dog, or perhaps something else: Could this be an attempt to make good on that threat?

So Frank and his colleagues begin to discover how the activists' engagement in anti-MTM activism has changed their lives. They avoid certain roads; they remove bumper stickers that might identify them as different; they even tell the sheriff about certain phone conversations. These threats transform everyday life into something that most people never have to consider: a "new normal" of heightened wariness that has distorted their lives so slowly that they have barely begun to recognize its consequences.

These activists are among the many stakeholders who have been involved in the conflict over MTM. Their reasons for becoming involved might include having an interest (in protecting the environment, for instance) or having something at risk (such as a job). For some, becoming involved is less a choice than a necessity. A delayed or revoked permit to mine may portend the loss of a job when other employment seems impossible. For others, the prospect of a mine encroaching on their home or their child's school evokes images of failed slurry ponds and battered landscapes that compel them to action. During the several decades of conflict over surface mining and now MTM, stakeholders and the groups they created and supported have pursued many activities to assert their interests: protesting, raising awareness, canvassing, lobbying, speaking out, joining lawsuits, and attending meetings and hearings.

Some of the leaders of the stakeholder groups working actively on MTM have become prominent and influential, such as the late Judy Bonds from Coal River Mountain Watch or Bill Raney from the West Virginia Coal Association. For many stakeholders, being involved in the conflict reflects an important personal commitment, despite the threats of violence, the slow progress, or the inconvenience; for some, the conflict has come to define who they are.

When an intense conflict deeply divides stakeholders, those who take active roles can feel pigeonholed into us-versus-them categories. Whether people are pro-MTM or anti-MTM comes to be the only information needed to determine how they should be treated. Yet as we pointed out in chapter 3, relationships among stakeholders can also be more nuanced and dynamic than those opposed categories would suggest. As this chapter shows, relationships within stakeholder groups and among them can shift in response to the tactics adopted by the individuals, groups, and institutions involved in the conflict and by the external forces, such as political and legal decisions, that shape the conflict.

The next two sections of this chapter focus on these concerns in one part of the coal-producing region: the Coal River watershed of West Virginia. The descriptions of stakeholders' activities along with a conflict assessment prepared about the region demonstrate the energy and resilience shown by some stakeholders, particularly those who identify with and participate in the local, regional, and national groups working on specific contentious issues. At the same time, these sections show how the complexity of the conflict over MTM and the deep divisions among those embroiled in it have made participation a painful and even dangerous pursuit for many stakeholders. A section titled "Federal Action Affects Stakeholders" describes how conflict dynamics shift when larger political entities become actively involved. Later sections of the chapter describe how the specter of violence has shaped the conflict dynamics and the relationships among stakeholders. Instances of violence in coalfields communities have captured the attention of several proponents of conflict resolution, who believe that a less adversarial approach might provide some relief, if not resolution. As the chapter recounts, several types of third-party intervention were contemplated and attempted, including efforts to bring stakeholders into meaningful deliberations.

Attempts to address violence directly or to address the underlying conflict can also alter relationships among stakeholders, for better or worse. As the chapter's concluding sections show, even with skilled third-party intervention, positive engagement among stakeholders can be difficult to achieve, especially when fear of violence has kept people from communicating with one another. Yet breakthroughs in communication and in relationships do happen. Careful and sensitive planning can lead to a breakthrough; but the same is true of other unexpected occurrences and even violence itself, which can result in change that transforms the conflict and stakeholders' relationships and perspectives.

Waves of Action, Antagonism, and Stalemate in the Coal River Valley

Throughout the 1990s, the pace of MTM continued to increase and to expand into new geographical areas of Appalachia. Not surprisingly, proposals to mine new mountains triggered fresh opposition to permits for mining and valley fills. In many instances, additional lawsuits and counter-suits were filed by MTM opponents (see, e.g., Burns 2007; Hufford 2003; Loeb 2007; Shnayerson 2008). The expansion of surface mining and the rise and persistence of litigation led more and more stakeholders to become involved.

Those opposed to MTM participated in local and regional stakeholder groups, such as the Ohio Valley Environmental Coalition, or formed new ones. Another option for participation was provided by national organizations that worked against the practice, such as the Sierra Club. For their part, Arch Coal, Massey Energy (now part of Alpha Natural Resources), and many other mining companies defended themselves in court, and the court of public opinion, while trying to maintain profitability and satisfy their workers and customers. Groups established to support the coal industry gained prominence, such as Friends of Coal (see friendsofcoal.org).

As stakeholders and stakeholder groups opposed to MTM were established and became increasingly visible and influential in the region, the dynamics of the conflict took new forms. It is difficult to generalize about the experiences of stakeholders in this large and complex conflict spanning multiple, diverse local communities; however, focusing on a small area yields a picture of waves of action, growing antagonism, stalemates, and rare shifts in conflict dynamics that many other communities have also experienced.

The Coal River runs north through Raleigh, Boone, and Kanawha Counties in southern West Virginia. Its two branches, the Little Coal River and the Big Coal River, meet and flow north toward the state capital, Charleston (for background on the area, see Aurora Lights n.d.; Hufford 2001). Route 3, part of which runs along the Big Coal River to the south and west of Coal River Mountain, passes by many features of the mining

FIGURE 4.1. A valley community near a mining site in the mountains, Fayette County, West Virginia.
Michael Sullivan.

industry, such as coal preparation plants, coal slurry ponds, active underground and surface mines, and closed or abandoned mines.

Residents living in the small towns and communities along Route 3, as well as in other areas of the Coal River watershed, have complained for years about coal company practices that degrade the air, streams, roads, and landscape. Eventually, some complaints made to environmental agencies or the courts were deemed to be violations that required coal companies to make amends and pay fines. But many complaints were simply ignored, determined to be without merit, or found to have no legal remedy.

In 1998 a grassroots organization called Coal River Mountain Watch (CRMW) was formed to call attention to the environmental impact of mining along Route 3 and elsewhere in the watershed and to counteract planned mountaintop mining and the valley fills that would accompany it. Permits issued or pending for surface mining would result in over five thousand acres mined using MTM techniques on Coal River Mountain, and sites for eighteen valley fills were identified. There were houses and recreation areas in the hollows that would be filled in, if permits were granted (Osha 2010).

Early in the first decade of the 2000s, Coal River Mountain was one of the few mountains in the area that had not yet been subjected to extensive surface mining or MTM. Concerned about shielding Coal River Mountain from destructive mining, the CRMW took on multiple issues and gained support from residents of coalfields communities, some of whom had become involved with regional groups working against MTM, such as the Ohio Valley Environmental Coalition (OVEC) and Kentuckians for the Commonwealth (see Hufford 2003). The goal for the CRMW and other advocacy groups—such as Mountain Justice, which began its activities in the area in 2005—was to stop MTM in the area by opposing permitting and demanding regulatory enforcement (see, e.g., Barry 2012; Burns 2007; Osha 2010; Shapiro 2010).

Stakeholders who organize to bring claims as a group generally achieve greater benefits than those who pursue issues on their own. Joining with others can lead to gaining recognition and attention for one's position, realizing camaraderie and emotional support, obtaining financial and logistical assistance, and being able to demonstrate that multiple people share the same concern—the upsides of stakeholder groups in a contentious conflict.

Yet organizing into groups can have negative effects on conflict dynamics, such as groupthink, isolation from other stakeholders, and hostility experienced in relationships with other groups. All these are routine, though not inevitable, effects of the formation of stakeholder groups during an intense and emotional conflict. One set of stakeholders might find that others have stereotyped them or demonized them, especially when they have had little interaction. For instance, almost anyone who expressed a view that questioned MTM was labeled a tree-hugger by the coal industry and other supporters of MTM, despite many community members never having had a previous affiliation with environmental causes. These downsides of organizing into stakeholder groups are often present, especially when stakeholders become deeply committed to a position in a conflict.

In 2005 a new group, Mountain Justice Summer (later, Mountain Justice), became prominent in the activities to save Coal River Mountain from

MTM. In her book on Mountain Justice, Tricia Shapiro describes how local activists began to work with Mountain Justice volunteers, many of whom had moved to the area to help call attention to the devastation of MTM. The Mountain Justice group acquainted local residents with strategies and tactics of nonviolent resistance, including direct actions against coal company interests. A broad mixture of activists joined in protests, occupations of coal company property, and disruptive participation at permitting hearings and other public gatherings (Shapiro 2010).

Mountain Justice group members were routinely criticized by many in the local communities, including some anti-MTM stakeholders who shared their goals. Primarily young people from outside the region and state, they were easily stereotyped as radical environmentalists, maybe even ecoterrorists, a task made easier because a few prominent members had been associated with such groups in the past. As Shapiro's *Mountain Justice* makes clear, the group members had a hard time disassociating themselves from the label of violent outsiders intruding into a local conflict. In fact, the group engaged in some activities that challenged property rights and, as the coal companies argued, endangered workers and themselves. As Shapiro makes clear, however, the public message of Mountain Justice was unqualified support for the use of nonviolent protest.

In 2006 and 2007 angry encounters between stakeholders with opposing views of MTM became more common in the Coal River watershed, and mining companies became more forceful in their refusal to allow their enterprise to be disrupted by protests, injunctions, and lawsuits. The tension rose to new levels, and reports of direct threats to activists were noted. At least one activist in the Coal River area began to wear a bulletproof vest; others tended to keep firearms or other protection nearby when at home or traveling. Stakeholders on all sides of the issue mounted security cameras on their property. Fear of violence became pervasive, especially for those stakeholders living in coalfields communities, and led some people in the region to avoid confrontation or any connection with those representing the "other side."

After a permit was granted for MTM on Coal River Mountain in 2006, additional legal challenges and direct action campaigns continued to ramp up. While the situation was tense and strained for local residents, other stakeholders—including coal operators, federal and state regulators, and investors—were feeling the debilitating effects of the seemingly endless lawsuits and countersuits, particularly over permitting, that created extreme uncertainty about the future of mining in the area. Of course, the backdrop to concerns over permitting was the competition from coal production in the western United States. The cycle of permit application, legal challenge, and response was wearing everyone down. This conflict had been building for over two decades without any end in sight, and many more stakeholders were involved by 2007 than at the start. Government regulators began to wonder if there was any way out of the waves of action, antagonism, and stalemate exacerbated by lawsuits, as well as any way to avoid violence.

Assessing the Situation in the Coal River Valley

At the center of the conflict over the Coal River Mountain area were concerns over regulatory policy and enforcement. In 2007 the EPA and regulators at the state level were actively involved but making little headway toward resolving any of the key issues. In recognition of the complexity and intractability of the conflict, including the many cases clogging the courts, and the intensity of encounters between people in local areas, the EPA's Conflict Resolution and Prevention Center along with its Region 3 office commissioned an assessment of the situation in the Coal River valley. The assessment was an effort by the EPA to consider a new approach to the conflict, perhaps one that could gain more agreement than anything else being attempted. The plan was for an independent third party to assess the conflict situation and determine whether collaborative processes could be developed and implemented to bring together key stakeholders to address MTM issues in less destructive, more productive ways. Although the assessment would focus on the Coal River valley, the regulators hoped that any recommendations produced could be used in other sites with similar conflicts in the coalfields region.

Situation assessments of this sort are commonly used in circumstances involving multiple parties, complex issues, public visibility, and a potential for violence. An assessment allows a convening agency, which typically sponsors such efforts, and other interested parties to be proactive in determining appropriate processes that address different stakeholder interests. The benefits of an assessment include identifying relevant parties, clarifying significant issues, identifying which issues should be addressed and which may be less important, and outlining an appropriate process.

The assessment in the Coal River valley was undertaken by the Keystone Center, a well-respected, nonprofit organization that specializes in consensus building and education, often in areas involving environment and science (Adler and Thompson 2008). As an independent third party, Keystone sought to engage a representative set of stakeholders in individual, open-ended interviews about their perspectives on MTM and the conflict. At the EPA's request, they took a watershed approach to identifying the stakeholders, which meant that they focused on stakeholders in one river valley, rather than on the variety of areas in the region where MTM was at issue. A watershed approach had the consequence of including stakeholders whose actions had immediate effects on one another through their common watershed. Yet it limited the issues to those that could be understood through that slice of the problem, and thus risked drawing conclusions for the region about a context that might be unique. Nevertheless, Keystone's research team, led by Doug Thompson, identified and interviewed seventeen stakeholders, including representatives from environmental organizations, state and federal regulatory agencies, and industry. The interviews addressed a range of issues, including the potential for determining the next steps for MTM in the watershed through a collaborative process that would bring stakeholders together.

Out of their interviews with these stakeholders, the research team identified three distinct approaches to the issues, which their report presents as "iconic stories" of the conflict.

- An industry narrative: Mountaintop mining is essential to the nation's energy strategy, should remain established in federal policy, and causes manageable environmental impacts.

- An environmental advocate narrative: Mountaintop mining is an environmentally disastrous, often unlawful practice destroying the natural and cultural landscape of the mid-Appalachian highlands.

- An on-the-ground perspective: Coal mining, for better and for worse, has always been and seemingly always will be part of our lives. (Adler and Thompson 2008, 8–9)

As the report maintains, these stark and contrasting positions are best viewed as points on a continuum that also includes more complex perspectives. The Keystone analysis goes on to assert that the issues at stake in the conflict tended to fall into three categories:

1. value concerns (e.g., protecting the environment or preserving mining culture)

2. factual issues (e.g., scientific studies of the impact of MTM)

3. legal questions (e.g., permitting authority)

Stakeholders expressed a range of perspectives on the issues underlying these three "frames" of the conflict, yet they all agreed that the status quo was untenable. Some expressed concern about increasing reports of violence and threats of violence. Opinions also diverged as to the worth of attempting a collaborative approach (Adler and Thompson 2008). Although lack of trust was seen as a barrier for some of those interviewed, others insisted that getting as many stakeholders as possible to the table was necessary to ensure the watershed's future.

The Keystone research team was committed to sharing the interview results with the stakeholders before finalizing the report, and they convened a meeting in Charleston, West Virginia, in August 2007. The meeting also allowed Keystone to bring the stakeholders together across lines of differences to observe how they would interact with one another. Those in attendance were asked to speak for themselves, rather than to speak as the representative of a group. Convener Doug Thompson expresses it this way: "Your hat is off, unless it's not." This ground rule frees participants to speak from their own expertise and experience and limits the need for anyone to represent a group position. When participants speak as individuals, the interaction is usually less formal and more open. However, this approach can pose a challenge for stakeholders who are used to speaking primarily on behalf of a group that might be their employer and might expect them to present a certain position.

The conversation among stakeholders at the August meeting showed genuine sincerity, albeit deep differences of perspective. They raised concerns about participating in a future collaborative process: Could they trust other stakeholders? Would ongoing litigation undermine their efforts? Would they lose legitimacy in their own groups by talking to the "other side," especially in a public forum? These and other concerns helped the research team develop recommendations that might be feasible under the circumstances.

The Keystone situation assessment identified four possible next steps that, if taken, could have a positive effect on the conflict: two different collaborative activities focused on landscaping and watershed planning, an interagency project to improve the climate for developing and enforcing fair regulation, and alternative dispute resolution approaches to resolve some of the legal disputes. Before describing the two collaborative activities that could bring together stakeholders in the Coal River valley, the authors of the situation assessment laid out multiple reasons that such collaboration might never take place, including the strong value commitments of stakeholders, especially environmentalists, and the industry's disincentive to collaborate. Yet the researchers also expressed the view that if all parties could be convinced of the potential for mutual gain and some, such as industry, could be persuaded to take a longer view, some collaboration could be effective.

Keystone's report acknowledged the extreme difficulty of convening a collaborative process in a situation in which stakeholders are deeply divided over the legitimacy of the practice of MTM itself. "Stop it immediately" or "Continue it indefinitely" were strong, diametrically opposed sentiments held by large constituencies, and neither side could see anything to be gained by compromising. Those who participated in the August discussion agreed that engaging in a collaborative process on some issues could be helpful, although the larger legal and policy issues would have to be decided through litigation and legislation.[1] Even for the skilled and experienced Keystone researchers, bringing people together in local communities seemed pretty difficult, given high tensions and the fact that the keys to definitive resolution lay outside the hands of those living closest to active mining sites.

Despite all their differences, the stakeholders interviewed by the Keystone team resembled one another in several ways. For one, they all insisted that the researchers would learn much from interviewing additional stakeholders, particularly the "local people," who, as each stakeholder insisted, would confirm their own pro- or anti-MTM perspective (cf. Osha 2010). Reflecting on the process several years later, Doug Thompson described his surprise at this reaction and yet understood it as evidence of just how separated the groups had become and, perhaps, how out of touch they were with the "other side." At the same time, almost all stakeholders saw themselves as victims. Industry believed that regulation was tighter in West Virginia than in surrounding states and that coal specifically was under attack by the current presidential administration. The environmentalists felt threatened by an industry that wielded considerable power and influence. If he had it to do over again, Thompson would interview a few more of the people who were positioned to play a role as bridge builders in the conflict, such as religious leaders or local politicians who might feel compelled to address the concerns of all their constituents.

Of the four options presented by Keystone, the only one ultimately pursued was a project to improve the efficiency and effectiveness of regulatory agencies (e.g., the EPA, the Army Corps, and others). Perhaps a limited budget or even a lack of political will precluded action on the other recommendations. Improving communication and clarifying relationships across the agencies proved to be a productive exercise, although, by that time, the role of federal regulators in the conflict was becoming increasingly controversial. As described in chapter 6, many stakeholders, sensing opportunity from a change in administration at the federal level from the Republican Party to the Democratic Party, became more proactive in taking their claims to Washington, DC.

When Conflict Heats Up

In the two years following Keystone's 2008 situation assessment, the pro-MTM and anti-MTM groups became more established, more entrenched, and more likely to encounter one another at confrontational public events focused on Coal River and other areas of Appalachia. The Coal River Mountain Watch continued to gain prominence through committed leaders such as Judy Bonds and Vernon Haltom, who pursued numerous actions to call attention to MTM and mining permit violations and plans. Mountain Justice and other emergent groups came to work alongside those who had been there for some time; activists from other parts of the United States joined in the struggle.

Often CRMW members and other activists were pitted against Massey Energy, which held permits for mines and valley fills in the area and was seeking new ones. The Massey Energy head, Don Blankenship, did not shy away from media attention; he defended MTM as a legitimate practice and vowed to continue mining for the good of Appalachia (Moyers 2007; see also the following box, on Massey/Alpha). Coal owners and operators broadcast their commitment to keep coal affordable for industry and consumers, to keep miners working, and to push back against any regulatory scrutiny that might slow them down.

Opponents of MTM were increasingly conscious of the broad and increasing extent of MTM in all the states in which it was being practiced, and efforts to challenge it pointed repeatedly to the scale of the enterprise. The intensity of the conflict was crystallized in diametrically opposed claims that either all the mountains would soon be blasted away or regulators would outlaw MTM entirely and thus obliterate Appalachia's economy. The war of words and actions was fierce.

Federal Action Affects Stakeholders

Some of the growing intensity in the conflict after 2007 was no doubt in reaction to uncertainty caused by the possibility of change at the top of the federal government. For all the stakeholders, the election of President Barack Obama, after eight years of George W. Bush's Republican administration, pointed to the likelihood of a new approach to MTM. A key factor would be changes in personnel and policy at EPA. The probability of a different approach was signaled early in the Obama administration when EPA head Lisa Jackson, an Obama appointee, announced in March 2009

Massey/Alpha

Before it was purchased by Alpha Natural Resources in 2011, Massey Energy (formerly A. T. Massey Coal Co.) was a major coal company with its roots in Appalachia and its headquarters in Richmond, Virginia. Massey Energy's mines (both underground and surface) and mining interests were spread throughout West Virginia and Kentucky. Over the last decades of the twentieth century, Massey was profitable and successful, as well as a major employer in the area.

But the company was also controversial. Massey endeavored to distinguish itself from other mining companies operating in the region. For instance, miners employed by Massey were rarely union members, and unionization was actively discouraged by managers and company bosses (see Brisbin 2002). Massey miners were easily identified by special, company-provided uniforms with red reflective stripes. The company's safety record was a cause for concern by some in the industry, and critics alleged that Massey put profits over the well-being of its employees.

After Appalachian-born Don Blankenship took over as CEO of Massey in 2000, complaints about safety and other company practices multiplied. Blankenship made no apologies about Massey's interest in making a profit and insisted repeatedly that coal-mining jobs had provided a good living for many families in the region. As Massey's pursuit of coal through MTM increased sharply in the 1990s, the company became the target of lawsuits and protests. Blankenship took a unique approach to being sued for violating labor, safety, and environmental regulations in that he directed company lawyers to contest all accusations in court and to file countersuits against critics. In a rare capitulation, in 2008 Massey paid a $20 million civil penalty—the largest ever—in a settlement related to the company's violation of the Clean Water Act provisions against discharging waste into streams and rivers.

Journalist Michael Shnayerson writes that under Blankenship, Massey had a reputation as "ruthless, relentless, and very aggressive" (Shnayerson 2008, 21), and Blankenship was a lightning rod for protestors against MTM.

that the agency would reconsider how permits for MTM were granted (Dickinson 2010; Eilperin 2009), and an action plan agreed to by three US federal agencies proposed eliminating the use of Nationwide Permit 21 (NWP 21) for surface mining (USACE, DOI, and EPA 2009). This opened up a public comment period, and hearings were scheduled throughout the coalfields region (USACE 2009).

But Blankenship's soft-spoken and even-tempered demeanor in public was an enigmatic counter to that ruthless image. The difficulties he had experienced growing up in poverty, and his rise to leadership through above-average intelligence and sheer hard work, also won him supporters. His softer side was also in evidence in the many times he presided over concerts, holiday celebrations, and charity giveaways held for the benefit of Massey employees and their families, although some people felt that he looked down on them (Goodell 2006).

The company seemed to lose its luster after a lethal explosion at its Upper Big Branch mine in April 2010 (Galuszka 2012). Under pressure from investors, Blankenship retired later that year, and Alpha Natural Resources took over in 2011. As a result of lawsuits against Massey, Alpha paid $210 million in damages, some of which went to the survivors of the Upper Big Branch disaster.

Alpha began in 2002 in Virginia, where it grew quickly. The company made efforts to build a reputation as environmentally conscious. Attention to sustainability and safety is prominent in its advertisements and Web presence; Alpha was the first coal company to build a natural stream channel at a mining site; previously most channels were lined with rocks, rather than allowing for the pools, streambed, and related habitat features of naturally occurring streams. The company philosophy is Running Right, which links protection for the environment with the following of safety guidelines. Former Alpha CEO Michael J. Quillen highlights his company's forward-looking perspective on energy: "Whether it's wind or solar or biomass, we try to get involved in those because not only are we interested in diversifying if it's right for the shareholders, but it's also educational. When we got into these green buildings, we learned the different categories of green building. . . . On sustainability, we've been working on that. . . . We were doing this before sustainability became a catchword" (Quillen 2010). Alpha's reputation for safety and for environmental awareness is better than Massey's, yet Quillen defends MTM as a practice whose end result can put a mountain back to "a higher and better standard."

One responsibility of the Army Corps is to ensure that US rivers and streams are not clogged with debris, and the Corps handles this through issuing permits that limit and control how a particular industry may discharge into a waterway. NWP 21 gives mine operators general permission to discharge the material that is a by-product of surface coal mining into streams and rivers without the need to conduct the studies required by an individual permit (USACE 2009; Fuschino 2007). With no efficient way to dispose of the rock, dirt, and other waste that results from coal mining (apart from dumping it into streams and rivers), the coal industry would face significant additional costs if the policy was changed. Under NWP 21, individual mine operators were not required to obtain permission from the Army Corps every time they sought to discharge mining by-product into rivers and streams (Fuschino 2007). The process of reviewing permit requests would offer the public an opportunity to comment on individual projects and possibly to object to them. Opponents of MTM had long targeted the permitting process as a way to slow the pace of surface mining in the region and to bring in public discussion on the conditions of specific mines and their potential for harm. Coal industry supporters, including miners, objected to any restrictions on permits and especially to environmental impact studies (EIS) and other reviews that would slow down and potentially hinder their ability to mine.

Some of the most contentious encounters between stakeholders occurred at public hearings organized by federal and state agencies. These hearings were intended to provide information about proposed changes to NWP 21 and other regulations related to mining as well as to collect public comments. Over the course of 2009, many stakeholder groups attended hearings; speaking out at those meetings and in other public settings was an increasingly important strategy in the MTM conflict. Some people were not used to stating their claims in public, and anti-MTM activists trained one another to present their position effectively. Coal companies urged their employees to attend hearings and rallies, so that the pro-MTM position would be articulated by working people both local and from outside the region. At several encounters in the spring and summer of 2009, concerns over the proposed changes to permitting fueled the anger with which stakeholders at all levels confronted one another.

Tension was in the air at the October 13, 2009, hearing on NWP 21 arranged by the Army Corps of Engineers in Charleston, West Virginia. The hearing was organized like others, with the main goal being to open the floor to public comment about what should happen to the permit. The hearing was concerned with two proposals: either to modify NWP 21 to prohibit it from applying to the Appalachian region, or to suspend NWP 21 while the Army Corps considered whether to eliminate it altogether

(USACE 2009). Neither action would stop discharges from taking place; rather, either modification or suspension would require a mine operator to request and obtain an individual permit before making any discharges.

As the stakeholders seeking to attend the hearing lined up outside and began to enter the auditorium, miners and anti-MTM activists expressed their positions loudly, and some hurled insults and threats. Anti-MTM activists were confronted by mining supporters who pushed them and effectively pinned them against a wall so that they could not get into the hearing (coalstories 2009). Security personnel, themselves vastly outnumbered, counseled the anti-MTM activists to leave for their own safety, and many did (Freeman 2009). The hearing proceeded.

The confrontation at the hearing was a watershed moment in the conflict, particularly for West Virginia stakeholders. Many people were outraged at the violence exhibited outside a public meeting organized and sponsored by government officials. Anti-MTM activists were especially angry, perhaps because they sensed that they might be getting closer to some of their goals and resented being held back precisely when gains finally seemed possible. Many organizations publicized the violence; the use of social media to reach broad constituencies revealed the tensions surrounding MTM and yet perhaps contributed to magnifying the importance of the threatening encounter. Some of the outrage was no doubt linked to the concern that violence could undermine the legitimacy of a public, democratic process, given that people representing one side of the issue were denied participation and effectively silenced. However, it was not as though public hearings had historically provided everyone an opportunity to be heard and this was an exception. Stakeholders on both sides were skeptical that such hearings had ever been effective; regardless of one's position, it often seemed as though no one in authority was really listening. But this hearing felt different, and the near violence of the hearing itself had effects on the next steps in the conflict at the local level and beyond.

Responding to Violence

To understand the role of threat and violence in the MTM conflict requires historical context. Violence and coal have a long, unhappy relationship. There are, of course, the death and injury that result from mining accidents, with thousands of such deaths every year around the world. There is the violence that occurs to miners who survive their careers underground only to succumb to black lung disease (pneumoconiosis) or related health problems. There is also the violence that occurs when retaining ponds fail or blasting goes awry. But most people, until recent years, associated violence with labor unions and coal companies. From the Molly Maguires, in the late 1800s, to Matewan and the Battle of Blair Mountain, in 1920 and 1921, to the Pittston strike over benefits, in 1989, confrontations between workers and owners have crossed the line into physical assault, sabotage, and outright shootings. With MTM, however, a new type of concern has emerged. The conflict over MTM has engendered many types of action; while mostly taking the legitimate forms of lobbying, organizing, protests and counterprotests, and public relations campaigns, instances of physical intimidation as well as substantial threats of violence have been made against many people, as the activists quoted in this chapter's opening vignette attest.

Besides the police investigations that any threat to public safety may bring about, these threats produced several less formal interventions, including efforts at conciliation, whereby a third party tries to lower the tensions among those embroiled in a conflict. One prominent approach to conciliation across deep divisions was already being pursued in West Virginia just after the violence at the hearing. Filmmaker Patrice O'Neill had come to West Virginia in early November 2009 for a series of presentations in Morgantown and Charleston about the organization called Not in Our Town (NIOT 2009). A pioneering approach to addressing instances of hatred and hate crimes, NIOT focuses on bringing community members together in discussion toward building hate-free communities where everyone can feel safe. Typically, NIOT intervenes when a community has experienced a glaring instance of hate-based violence or discrimination. Out of concern over the increasing threat of violence due to the MTM conflict, including the incident at the permit hearing, Paul Sheridan, an attorney in the West Virginia attorney general's office with a record of combating hate crime, arranged a meeting between O'Neill and anti-MTM activists who had received death threats. From all accounts the meeting went well. Although conversations stimulated by NIOT can be reassuring and inspiring for people who experience threat, and can lead to initiatives that prevent future violence, the polarization in communities can stubbornly persist. This was the case in the coalfields communities, and as 2009 came to a close, the fear that other violence might break out was palpable.

The turbulence at the NWP 21 hearing and other threats of violence expressed in public and private settings also generated one of the few attempts to bring parties to the MTM conflict together to talk about how they might resolve their differences. Once again, it was the West Virginia attorney general's office that helped set up the meeting, but it took the good offices of country music star Kathy Mattea and the political clout of West Virginia's governor to get the deeply opposed parties to agree to come to the table for a mediated discussion.

In January 2008 Governor Joe Manchin and his wife welcomed to their home a small group comprising top figures in the conflict over MTM. Among those present were OVEC organizer Maria Gunnoe; Coal River Mountain Watch codirector Vernon Haltom; Governor Manchin's policy adviser, Jim Pitrolo; Ted Hapney, with the United Mine Workers of America; Rev. Dennis Sparks, executive director of the West Virginia Council of Churches at the time; and Si Kahn, a musician with a long history of social activism (OVEC 2010b). A professional mediator led the conversation, but it was clear that Kathy Mattea, out of concern over MTM and over the violence of the conflict, had been instrumental in convening the conversation and providing the inspiration to help those embroiled in conflict reach out to one another.

Participants agreed to keep the specifics of the conversation confidential, especially from the media, and little is known about what was actually said. Reports of the general tone of the discussion note that those in attendance spoke of their grave concern over the growing threat of violence in the coalfields communities. They talked as well about persistent, deep divisions among people, including within families, who were strained to the breaking point. Governor Manchin was asked what he was willing to do to help address these and other issues. The limited media accounts indicate that the governor listened intently and stayed longer than many had expected. Dinner was brought in, and even after the Manchins retired for the evening, the assembled stakeholders continued talking. Many of the individuals in the room besides the mediator had experience in facilitating heated conversations and kept the session from breaking down. For instance, in his position as head of the West Virginia Council of Churches, Sparks had experience mediating considerable controversy over many issues, including MTM (Hamill 2010; see box on Dennis Sparks).

The participants at the meeting held at the governor's mansion expressed different opinions about what their gathering had accomplished. One notable limitation was that some key stakeholder groups were not represented. For instance, Bill Raney of the West Virginia Coal Association had been invited to participate on behalf of the coal industry but was unable to attend. The perspectives of those who work in the mines were expressed primarily by a union representative. Some attendees wished that they could have spoken directly with industry representatives or miners, while others believed that their absence opened an opportunity to communicate more freely with the governor.

Getting the governor's attention was an undeniably important achievement of the meeting. Governor Manchin, a former coal operator whose public stands placed him strongly in favor of mining and against tightening mining regulations, was an unlikely candidate to serve as a conciliator. For months, activists in the Coal River area had been asking to meet with Manchin and his staff to request help in relocating Marsh Fork Elementary School and stopping the expansion of MTM on Coal River Mountain (Shapiro 2010). Perhaps by coincidence or perhaps by design, the governor met with a group of those residents the day after the private mediation at his home (OVEC 2010a, 2010b). One participant speculated that the governor saw the first meeting as a way of preparing for the second, which he knew would be contentious. The second meeting included politicians as well as many key stakeholders in the MTM conflict. After the discussions, some of these stakeholders made statements, as did Governor Manchin and Kathy Mattea. The governor reaffirmed his commitment to MTM and other forms of mining, which he depicted as crucial to maintaining West Virginia's economy.

Dennis Sparks

A commitment to working against violence has motivated the Reverend Dennis Sparks to position himself as a conciliator and mediator in various conflicts. As a pastor in Charleston, West Virginia, he has dealt with violence associated with the drug trade, mining disasters, crushing rural and urban poverty, and the conflict over MTM. During eight years as head of the West Virginia Council of Churches (WVCC), Sparks led his group into the center of the MTM conflict, when the WVCC called for strict enforcement of the laws regulating MTM. Sparks defends the WVCC's position, while acknowledging that he and his group took a "hard walk" (Hamill 2010). The influential group had to balance a belief that Christians should practice good stewardship of earthly resources with a concern that limits on mining could lead to job losses. Weighing the options, they chose to protect the environment and the health of coalfields residents. Difficult choices, complex conflicts, and contentious conversations are Reverend Sparks's forte, and he has engaged in all three in his work on controversial public-policy issues. Sparks credits his success on some issues (e.g., raising awareness about gambling addiction) to the strong relationships he has with a wide range of people, including those whose views he does not share. For instance, he surprised some people, and angered others, by working with officials from the coal association and miners' union to pass and enforce laws protecting cemeteries from industrial damage.

Much as Reverend Sparks succeeds in bringing stakeholders together to talk through difficult issues and problems, he also has a reputation for communicating hard realities, telling people—including powerful people—things they would rather not hear. Sparks speaks up until politicians and industry officials are forced to confront, and sometimes admit, the suffering experienced by people who live and work in mining areas.

Sparks's ability to be heard, and to compel others to act, comes not only from his own trustworthy demeanor but also from his hard work on behalf of miners. Well before taking its stance against MTM, the WVCC under Sparks had begun to play a key role in assisting state and local authorities after coal-mining disasters. WVCC members provided food and shelter, transportation, and logistics, especially for families mourning a loved one. Sparks knew he was capable of making a difference on contentious issues involving coal when Bill Raney, head of the West Virginia Coal Association, stopped him at the state capitol, where they had each gone to address concerns about potential violence between miners and anti-MTM activists. Raney said, "Sit down, Preacher, we need to talk about working together." Out of compassion for communities living under the threat of violence, Reverend Sparks urged Governor Manchin to host the conciliatory conversation that would bring together anti-MTM activists with representatives of miners. In Sparks's estimation, the conversation succeeded in raising awareness about violence in the coalfields and the need for communication among those stakeholders with the power to prevent it.

FIGURE 4.2. A press conference with Governor Manchin, politicians, and activists.
Charleston Gazette/Chip Ellis.

Following the meetings, Governor Manchin released a statement
calling for "calm in the coalfields" (Ward 2010a). Writing on his blog *Coal
Tattoo,* journalist Ken Ward Jr. reported, "Manchin emerged from a long
meeting with coalfield citizens and issued a call for an end to threats and
intimidation against West Virginians who are fighting to stop mountaintop removal: 'We will not in any way, shape or form in this state of West
Virginia tolerate any violence against anyone on any side. If you're going
to have the dialogue, have respect for each other'" (Ward 2010a). The governor's condemnation of violence was especially welcome news for several
activists who were engaged in a "tree sit" on mine company property. The
coal company's use of deafening noisemakers to try to force the activists
down from the trees could hardly be carried out after the call for calm and
the direct intervention of the governor's office (Shapiro 2010).

In the aftermath of the mediation, meetings, and the governor's an-
nouncement, some key stakeholders had the sense that additional discussions or mediations might be possible. But it proved difficult to bring
stakeholders concerned about the Coal River area together again, across
the divisions that Doug Thompson's team had found when they conducted

the situation assessment several years earlier. Those divisions had only deepened as both sides continued to sue and countersue over permitting and other issues and to engage in direct actions and combative media campaigns. As Jen Osha put it in her study of local responses to MTM in the Coal River Mountain area, "Since the beginning of 2009, there has been a steady upwelling of direct, non-violent civil disobedience to stop mountaintop removal and raise awareness about the dangers of slurry impoundments" (Osha 2010, 63).

Although the executives from coal companies and utilities routinely hold meetings with politicians, including Governor Manchin and other politically and economically powerful stakeholders in the MTM conflict (e.g., investors and developers), coal executives rarely get directly involved in discussing MTM with residents living near the mines and with environmental activists (OVEC 2010a). This is not surprising, as stakeholders who control the greatest assets often see no reason to take steps that might indicate compromise of their position. Able to withstand the pressure of protests, negative media campaigns, and direct actions from other stakeholders, the coal executives prefer to continue their business as usual and respond in court to any challenges.

With long experience in conflict resolution, Doug Thompson of the Keystone Center affirms that people who hold positions of power generally have a hard time giving anything up or taking a step toward bridging deep differences. Yet this puzzles him: Why is it so difficult for people in power to see that their position might be the very best one from which to offer or accept a conciliatory gesture? What's especially puzzling is that powerful stakeholders often fail to realize or admit that power relations can change. Were those in power able to imagine different circumstances in the future, ones in which they were less advantaged, they might come to the table, if only to protect their interests. The history of economic ups and downs in the region offers a vivid cautionary tale about the likelihood of change for the worse. Yet perhaps in 2010 the changes at the federal level had already caused the most powerful stakeholders to feel that their fortunes might be shifting in unanticipated and unwelcome ways.

The lives of many stakeholders in the MTM conflict changed suddenly and drastically on April 5, 2010. On that date a devastating explosion went off deep inside the Upper Big Branch underground mine in Montcoal, West Virginia.[2] Community members and Mountain Justice activists living on Coal River Road knew something terrible had happened when they heard siren after siren as vehicles sped up Coal River Road toward hospitals in Beckley, the closest major town. Families of miners gathered to wait for news of efforts to recover the bodies of those killed and perhaps to rescue the four miners still unaccounted for after the blast. Fumes in the mine hampered the rescue process and made the situation extremely painful for those who waited to learn the fate of loved ones trapped in the mine. After several days, rescuers located the bodies of the four missing men, and the death toll rose to twenty-nine. The disaster at Upper Big Branch mine was the country's deadliest coal-mining incident in forty years (Galuszka 2012).

As a result of the deaths at Upper Big Branch mine, relationships among stakeholders in the MTM conflict changed abruptly; former opponents reached out to help one another and provide assistance. The Reverend Dennis Sparks, Massey CEO Don Blankenship, and Bill Raney from the Coal Association found that, despite their deep opposition over MTM, they needed to work together to offer information and comfort to families who looked to them for help and leadership.

The disaster affected everyone along Coal River Road and throughout the coalfields. The suffering experienced by families and the community as a result of the explosion and deaths reminded everyone of the dangers of mining but also of the resilience of people who come together in moments of crisis.

The tragedy led some activists to redouble their efforts against coal companies, especially Massey Energy and its CEO, Don Blankenship; those who railed against coal mining as exploitative of workers would eventually have plenty of evidence for their claims that the mining companies cared more about profits than for the miners and their communities, as ultimately the operators at Upper Big Branch would be found guilty of criminal negligence and other charges (see box on Massey/Alpha, above). Some anti-MTM activists worried that this incontrovertible evidence of the risks of underground mining made MTM look like a safer option. The extensive media presence in the Coal River area meant that the MTM conflict received some national attention, although the main story was the Upper Big Branch blast and its aftermath, during which the criminality of working conditions at the mine began to come to light.

One prominent activist found that, after the Upper Big Branch disaster, she had difficulty working on the front lines of the movement against MTM, especially confronting miners and their families. Lorelei Scarbro still opposed MTM yet expressed the need to work even more concertedly toward positive, future-oriented goals. She put additional energy into increasing the capacity for wind power in the very mountains slated for blasting by Massey Energy (*Coal River Mountain* 2008; Scarbro 2009, 2010).

The interest in using the mountaintops for wind power, which was shared by some (but not all) environmental activists, reflects not only a move toward alternative forms of energy but also an effort to develop new economic opportunities for the region's workforce. Embracing wind farms and other enterprises to enhance Appalachian economic development "beyond coal" was beginning to emerge in other parts of the coalfields, too, as the next chapter describes.

In June 2010, after many hearings and public presentations, the Army Corps announced that it would suspend NWP 21 (USACE 2010), and many stakeholders scrambled to figure out what that decision might mean for the future of MTM. Those opposed to MTM were cautiously optimistic. For their part, the coal industry swiftly condemned the Army Corps's action as the latest salvo in the Obama administration's "war on coal" (Reid 2010). Almost immediately, the suspension of NWP 21 was challenged in court, and the back and forth of litigation began anew. Fights over NWP 21 and several related issues involving permits and procedures ensured that the future of MTM would remain uncertain and contested. We return to this topic in chapter 6.

FIVE

Building Consensus among Stakeholders

The entrance of a large group into the Harvest Table Restaurant in Meadowview, Virginia, raises some eyebrows around the room, although most diners are too polite to stare. This group is energized, and not only because of the presence of two engaging youngsters at one of their two tables. They have made their way from St. Paul, Virginia, where some ninety minutes earlier they had facilitated a meeting of the Clinch River Valley Initiative (CRVI). Everyone, including the two authors of this book, thought the meeting had gone very well. Some of the graduate students from the Institute for Environmental Negotiation (IEN) at the University of Virginia have been working on this initiative for a year, but given the distance between Charlottesville and southwestern Virginia, the visits to the region had been infrequent and treasured occasions.

A meeting of this sort, which in fact was several meetings at once (a CRVI steering committee meeting, a general meeting, breakout sessions for action groups, and a final reconvening of the whole group), takes a lot of coordination. A date that works for most people must be set, planning documents updated, the facility reserved, announcements sent out, food and drink arranged, agendas prepared, speakers confirmed, sign-in table set up, name tags and markers made available, projector connected and tested, chairs and tables positioned properly, small-group facilitators and recorders assigned, flip chart stands and paper placed with each breakout group, and checks written to the caterer and host. The immediate aftermath may only be a little less busy, with quick check-ins with participants, the room rearranged, food cleaned up, recycling hauled away, small-group notes collected, and farewell hugs and handshakes given.

The discussion at dinner is all about the meeting and the CRVI project. CRVI has many moving parts. There is excitement about a planned education summit for later in the year, assessment of the progress made in developing a hoped-for state park, delight at the prospect of additional access points along the river, and confirmation of the need to get people out on the Clinch River in canoes and kayaks during the next meeting.

The cofacilitators, Frank Dukes and Christine Gyovai, make an effort to debrief even as Christine feeds her two youngsters, brought to dinner by her spouse and mother-in-law. Did we prepare well? Did we miss something? Did anyone leave upset? What should our next steps be?

As dinner breaks up, around eight in the evening, the group faces a downpour and another four hours of driving before reaching Charlottesville. But nobody complains about the long trip; it will allow for more debriefing and planning for future activities.

This chapter describes the effort by one of the authors, Frank, to intervene in the coalfields as a consensus builder in what has come to be called the Clinch River Valley Initiative (CRVI). The chapter looks at why this effort is being made and how the effort has shaped stakeholder interests and relationships in southwestern Virginia. The lively meeting of CRVI described above was the seventh such meeting out of a total of thirteen as of this book's publication. Only a year before, CRVI did not exist. The chapter begins with Frank's approach to consensus building, and subsequent sections tell the story of how Frank and his colleagues used it to bring stakeholders together.

An Approach to Consensus Building

Consensus building connotes an effort that seeks to build widespread legitimacy among stakeholders for changes in policy and practices. In contrast to mediation and conciliation, as described in chapter 3, consensus building has goals that are long term and wide in scope, and they generally require support from a broader community than the immediate stakeholders themselves.

Consensus decision making has a long history in indigenous peoples' practices as well as in some faith communities, most prominently the Quaker Meeting. As a practice of environmental conflict resolution, consensus building has a history dating back over three decades, with a substantial body of research and practice (see, e.g., Dukes 2004; Susskind and Thomas-Larmer 1999). Consensus building is characterized by the following qualities:

- direct, face-to-face discussions among the parties
- a focus on deliberation that is intended to enhance participants' mutual education and understanding
- inclusion of multiple sectors representing diverse and often conflicting perspectives

- openness and adaptability of the process
- agreement among all the parties as the basis for decisions, or some variation other than majority decision making (Dukes 2004)

The consensus-building process need not be led by a third party without an active stake in the issues, although that is a common practice in the environmental arena. Most consensus-building efforts use a formal consensus rule that all parties must support all major decisions. Several reasons for this rule about decision making reflect a concern for developing constructive relationships among stakeholders:

- Participants who will have some responsibility for implementing agreements need a say in those decisions, or they will be more likely to oppose them.

- It is important to get all parties to the table; individual participants who might be skeptical of working with opponents or those they don't know can be reassured by having effective veto power over any decisions.

- Group members know that they need to attempt to satisfy the needs of all participants, a requirement that changes the group dynamics from a majoritarian effort to one in which everyone's concerns must be addressed.

- Minority views that may have otherwise been summarily dismissed need to be given real consideration.

- A norm of group caring and responsibility may be enhanced. (Dukes 2006)

As a practical matter, decisions with broad-based support are more likely to be implemented faster and more thoroughly.

Consensus building often combines the elements of common public outreach (such as public meetings, mailings, and news releases) with meetings involving a stakeholder decision group that convenes over an extended period of time. Such groups typically have a defined membership and a clear purpose and goals, and they employ the tools of dialogue and deliberation.

Consensus building that is inclusive and enduring, and that generates successful actions, also builds community trust, partnerships, knowledge, and social and political capital (Innes 1999), which are important community benefits.

FIGURE 5.1. Potential of authentic collaboration.
E. Franklin Dukes.

Consensus-Building Theory and Practice in Southwestern Virginia

One of the authors of this volume, Frank, has been engaged for some time with efforts to intervene as a third-party consensus builder in the coalfields where MTM is contested. These efforts do not engage directly with the question of whether MTM should continue or not; rather, they address several underlying issues involving the environment and the economy. Such an approach reflects the reality at publication time: a consensus about the future of MTM is virtually impossible, and any effort to develop such a consensus among the key parties would most likely achieve little and might even be harmful by raising unrealistic hopes.

A number of companies practice MTM, and many different interests support and oppose it. Why would the parties agree to come to the table to discuss the possibility of ending MTM? Imagine, if you will, a voluntary agreement that might include some time frame in which MTM continues to occur at a gradually reduced level before being brought to a halt. Why would a company engaged in a profitable practice agree to an arrangement that would likely reduce its profitability and cause it to default on its obligation to its stockholders? Conversely, why would any community or environmental advocacy group in effect sell out those communities that would continue to be subject to MTM in this interim period? Imagine the leadership of each constituency attempting to explain to its members such an agreement; they would not remain in a leadership position for long.

Despite the realistic appraisal by Adler and Thompson (2008) that no agreement about the future of MTM is possible among the key stakeholders—an appraisal endorsed by the authors as well—considerable activity in the coalfields toward consensus building and conflict resolution addresses the issues that the conflict over MTM reveals. This activity is centered around another option that might slow or even halt MTM. That effort, in short, is to make the mountains too valuable a resource to destroy and the rivers and streams too important to risk harming. An increasing number of anti-MTM activists endorse this approach and use it with the goal of changing the working assumption that removing substantial portions of the mountains and filling streams provide greater economic benefits than does preserving the mountains and streams. This effort currently takes two forms: development of wind power along the mountain ridges; and development within the region of a wider, more resilient economic base, including entrepreneurialism for small businesses and tourism focused on cultural heritage and recreational attractions, such as hiking, rafting, fishing, canoeing, and kayaking. The promotion of wind power is occurring in a number of areas and is not without its own controversy within the environmental-advocacy movement. But efforts related to the second option include an array of interventions designed to address the economic, ecological, and social challenges of the region, including the initiative called Appalachian Transition.[1]

One of the most substantial of these efforts is taking place in the coalfields of southwestern Virginia. This project began informally with the theme of Building Local Economies and has since become the Clinch River Valley Initiative. As is often the case in such efforts, this consensus-building project resulted from a confluence of timeliness, circumstance, relationship, and initiative.

Frank had been pondering for a few years whether and how there might be a role for the type of facilitated consensus building offered by the Institute for Environmental Negotiation, which he directs. He had found the juxtaposition of interdependence, paradox, and challenge that MTM brings compelling for many reasons, not least because this issue takes place within his home state and neighboring states. He saw many parallels to work he had done for seven years with tobacco-farming communities and public-health advocates. One finds many paradoxes in the region: substantial reliance on the economic value of coal even as its extraction brings such visible human and environmental costs; widespread poverty and its by-products, particularly health problems, in the midst of such rich and beautiful natural resources; and the power and endurance of Appalachian culture, with both strengths and disadvantages. Furthermore, the conflict over MTM had begun to produce threats, intimidation, and the risk of violence, and Frank came to believe that bringing together some of the key stakeholders might reduce the amount of antagonism and lower the threat of violence.

But there did not seem to be any clear path to gaining entry into this arena; nobody was beating down the doors of his institute asking for assistance. So he began looking for an approach that might prove valuable to those in this region who are affected so powerfully by MTM and related issues.

He found that entry through the Virginia Natural Resources Leadership Institute (VNRLI), a nine-month program that since 1999 has brought together a diverse group of environmental leaders (VNRLI Fellows) from business, nonprofit, and public sectors to learn conflict resolution and collaboration and their applicability to Virginia's environmental issues. This powerful program challenges misconceptions about the "other" typically held by stakeholders in the sectors mentioned above, showcases examples of successful consensus-building efforts throughout the state, and features contemporary conflicts as case studies that encourage VNRLI Fellows to think about the sources, dynamics, and potential means of resolution and transformation of the issues. In 2009, as part of the VNRLI annual visit to the coalfields of southwestern Virginia, Frank decided to highlight tensions over energy and electricity, as manifested by a recently approved, highly controversial coal-fired power plant being built in the region, as well as by MTM. To do so he and his colleagues hosted a facilitated discussion with a stakeholders' panel addressing the two dozen or so VNRLI Fellows.

Convening a panel on such controversial issues requires more than the usual amount of preparation. Stakeholders often have deep concerns about how they will be treated. They may never before have engaged their opponents in such close proximity. They may wonder whether there is a hidden agenda that could result in harm to their cause or that might make for a very uncomfortable experience. Many who have spent time in the public eye have become wary of seeing their views distorted in print or challenged by audience members (in this case, the VNRLI Fellows). Sometimes individuals refuse to participate in such forums because of these concerns.

Some stakeholders, however, welcome the opportunity to enlarge their audience and make their case, even as they may still have anxiety about participating. In this situation, Frank and his associates were able to convene a panel consisting of an administrator from the state agency that oversees mining regulations, a regional economic development official, a representative of the controversial coal-fired power plant under construction, and two environmental activists well known as opponents of MTM, one of whom is native to the region. Because the VNRLI Fellows were to follow the panel with a visit to an active coal mine that would demonstrate MTM, Frank was less concerned than he otherwise would have been that the panel did not include a coal industry representative.

The discussion proceeded as such panels often do: with interest from the audience and, to the panelists' relief, a good bit of civility. Each panelist was allowed to speak without interruption before questions from the moderator (Frank) or the fellows took place. The VNRLI Fellows demonstrated genuine curiosity about many issues and peppered the panelists with questions that the stakeholders were glad to answer. Panelists were even-tempered but direct and, at times, passionate in expressing their views as stakeholders. They gradually became more comfortable with the situation as they realized that they were not going to be attacked and that they would be allowed to say exactly what they wanted to say.

Following the session, Frank took the panelists to a private room for a debriefing over lunch. Participants were relieved, even energized, as they shared their concerns and hopes with one another and expressed how much they got out of the session. Despite their continuing differences, they could identify specific issues that they believed might offer not only common ground but also significant potential alliances, such as cleaning up

waste from coal production and promoting wind energy. And the panelists agreed, when one of them commented, "We should be talking like this
every month." Thus began a slow, careful process of intervention toward
consensus building among stakeholders.

The CRVI Consensus-Building Process

At the Institute for Environmental Negotiation, Frank and his colleagues speak of three phases of any consensus-building process: *conceiving*
the process, *conducting* the process, and *completing* the process. This heuris-
tic allows them not only to break down what could seem an overwhelm-
ingly complex project into more readily understood components; it helps
them communicate to the stakeholders that process design (conceiving the
process) is on a par with conducting the meetings themselves. It also highlights the importance of working with the end (completing the process) in
mind from the very beginning of a project.

While distinct actions are associated with each phase, those actions do
not always proceed in a linear fashion, but may be iterative instead. That is,
throughout the consensus-building process the third-party facilitators—
in this case, Christine Gyovai (see box on Gyovai) and Frank—and participants need to adapt to developments among those participants as well as
the conditions external to the process. Thus, during the conducting phase,
facilitators may continually remind participants of the need to consider
how their work would be implemented (or "completed") and adopt appropriate changes to the process ("conceiving" its design) in order to meet their
goals. Examples during CRVI have included inviting new participants to
join an action group, briefing elected officials, and seeking funding from a
newly available source.

Conceiving the process includes the key activities of conducting a
situation assessment, designing a proposed process, and inviting the appropriate participants. This phase is characterized by strategic thinking
and adaptive planning and may include an initial scoping meeting where
all parties would review the issues and the proposed process. The Clinch
River Valley Initiative took this approach, but much work preceded the
scoping meeting.

Christine Gyovai

Although only in her thirties, Christine Gyovai has been facilitating environmental issues for over a decade. She frequently speaks on topics such as permaculture design and creating sustainable communities throughout the mid-Atlantic, and she cofacilitates trainings around sustainability, facilitation, and collaborative problem solving.

A self-professed homesteader in central Virginia with two young children, she brings her passion for community self-determination and empowerment to her work in the coalfields. She notes that "it's really different than a lot of the facilitation work that I do, where I really don't go into my personal background; but in this work that's the first thing I talk about, my family. My grandfather was a coal miner, my great-grandfather was a coal miner in southern West Virginia." Making that connection has an impact on how people engage with her.

Christine grew up in West Virginia and has been concerned about the region for a long time. She has been thinking about how communities can actively shape their own destinies; she and her husband, also from West Virginia, made a film about MTM while in graduate school. She takes great care to acknowledge the importance of coal to so many in the region, including her own family, while acknowledging the scope of the impacts of MTM on the landscape as well as on local social and economic systems.

Christine sees her facilitative role as providing a space for people to talk about issues and, beyond that, a place for folks to ask, What do we want to consciously cultivate in the community? How do we envision and create what we want for our community? How do we talk about what we want to sustain? She admires the work of those who find ways to celebrate culture, even as they look for diverse ways to sustain themselves economically. Among the most enjoyable tasks associated with CRVI has been to record recollections of residents in the region, as a way of connecting the past to the future. She also advocates for the engagement of youth and educators in CRVI, as well as in other collaborative efforts.

She notes that an economy based on the Clinch River cannot be outsourced to another country the way that a call center in southwest Virginia recently was. Her work with CRVI allows her to integrate her many interests, even as she occasionally wonders if meeting the needs of communities struggling to get by requires efforts beyond her role as a facilitator. Connecting directly with community members is one of her great joys in working with CRVI.

SITUATION ASSESSMENT

Before beginning a project in a situation involving complexity and expense, a sponsoring organization generally conducts a thorough assessment of stakeholders' needs, interests, and concerns (see, e.g., Bean, Fisher, and Eng 2007; Susskind and Thomas-Larmer 1999). Many situation assessments are conducted at considerable expense using sophisticated interviewing techniques. The Adler and Thompson (2008) assessment is a prime example of such work (see chapter 4). However, some circumstances may not allow for a formal assessment. In Frank's case, no convening body was seeking such a report, and he had no deadline to compel its completion and no budget to pay for the assessment. Frank and Christine began with informal interviews; after actually convening the parties, they followed up with a more systematic and complete assessment.

Good practice allows for flexibility in planning how such assessments are conducted. The sensitive nature and high stakes of such issues, varying levels of interest and knowledge, and different roles of stakeholders make it essential to be flexible in the questions asked and the type of interview used. For some people with little at stake or limited time, interviews by telephone may be appropriate; for others a face-to-face meeting may be essential to ensure an accurate understanding. For issues as sensitive as they are in the coalfields, direct personal contact has been important in the development of the CRVI project.

An equally important aspect of the assessment that Frank and Christine conducted is how the third-party intervener may earn the trust of the key parties and build legitimacy for the intervention (see Bean, Fisher, and Eng 2007). During the first two years of this intervention, Frank and Christine used all the methods described below, as well as a review of newspaper and journal articles, to help them gain an understanding of the situation and build sufficient relationships of trust for their intervention to gain legitimacy:

- the annual panels and site visits in the region of the Virginia Natural Resources Leadership Institute (the initial panel as described earlier)
- in-person, focused meetings in the coalfields with individuals and small groups
- individual and conference calls with key stakeholders
- graduate-class projects that supported stakeholders' interests[2]
- discussions before, during, and after each meeting related to the project

Interview questions, crafted individually for each situation, are intended to allow an assessment team to answer more general questions:

+ Who are the parties engaged in the issues? What is their current role? What has been their role in the past? What goals do they have?

+ Who has authority over which aspects of the issues? Is there any formal or informal leadership group looking at any of these issues, and if so, who do they represent? Who is left out of the decision process, and why?

+ What are the differences in views among the most important stakeholders? Within the community at large?

Typically, upon completion of the interviews, a report is compiled that summarizes the interests, needs, and concerns of the interviewees. That information is used to suggest ways that the interested parties might engage one another; those options may range from no action, to a limited dialogue, to a full consensus-building process, as was the case in the process that led to CRVI. Depending on the sensitivities of the issues, a report can be written or oral, and interviewees' requests for confidentiality are honored by promising that specific comments will not be attributed to any individual or organization. Frank and Christine certainly have had many confidential conversations with stakeholders as CRVI emerged; the written report maintains confidentiality. Like other reports it includes a list of interviewees and indications of needs, concerns, and interests by individual, organization, and stakeholder category.

CONCEIVING THE PROCESS

Based on the understanding gained through the assessment, including dozens of conversations with key stakeholders, by the summer of 2010 Frank and Christine had concluded that an intervention was warranted and possible. But intervention to do what? Issues that various stakeholders in West Virginia and Virginia identified were geographically and topically diverse. They could have included restoring landscapes at mined sites; cleaning up mine waste; developing other forms of energy, including wind and biomass; and expanding traditional tourism as well as ecotourism and the "creative economy,"[3] which focuses on small businesses marketing arts, crafts, and music native to the region. A wonderful example of this is Abingdon, Virginia's Heartwood Center, directed by Todd Christensen.

Todd Christensen

Todd Christensen introduces himself as a community developer, and one quickly realizes that he lives and breathes that role. He wears many hats in his job in the Virginia Department of Housing and Community Development: he manages the community development block grant program for the state, he plays a similar role for Virginia's share of Appalachian Regional Commission grants, and he heads the Heartwood Center, a twenty-nine-thousand-square-foot cultural center in Abingdon showing the finest of Appalachian arts and crafts and featuring local music and local food.

Todd realizes that nobody wants to live in a community where the downtown is full of empty storefronts. But he also relates how he woke up one day to realize that one could make everything physically perfect downtown, with buildings and homes rehabilitated, and the town could still have 20 percent unemployment. Nonetheless, traditional economic development was insufficient. For example, along with many others, he had worked to bring in a call center in an industrial park whose development had cost millions of dollars; when the call center closed, the jobs and investment disappeared completely.

According to Todd, the secret tragedy of every rural place in America is the loss of youth who find too little to keep them home—too little recreation and social life, too little employment. This has to be a place where twenty-five-year-olds want to live.

So he and others began rethinking their role. Eventually, he and his colleagues and partners gathered many people together to create a heritage music trail that became the Crooked Road. Former Virginia governor Mark Warner wanted to do something similar for crafts, so they began 'Round the Mountain to do just that. People laughed at their vision to make the area an international tourist destination, but a decade later it was well on the way to becoming one.

Todd sees their focus as building viable communities, by which he means fostering quality of life, creating a sense of place, focusing on unique natural assets and experiences; in short, providing places where people want to live. This also means supporting an entrepreneurial infrastructure, such as putting in fiber optics systems to attract people who could run their businesses in the region.

One of his biggest fears is losing what makes the area unique. He makes clear that while this looks like tourism, and smells like tourism, it's not exactly tourism. They don't want to become a Dollywood, catering to tourists seeking glitz and glamour. Instead, they have more children playing traditional music in schools than one can imagine. They want to be a region where every place has a story, where everyone can have an interesting experience. It also needs to be a place that values its natural resources, where outdoor recreation is popular and easily accessible.

The question of focus for an intervention is best put to the residents and leadership in the area itself. What interests stakeholders? To answer that question, Frank and Christine needed to move beyond meetings and calls with a small number of people to bring together differing and sometimes competing interests to determine if the consensus-building effort could move to an active phase of deliberation. With the hope of continuing to develop an authentic, enduring project, they decided to concentrate on one geographic region: southwestern Virginia's coalfields.

The next step was to convene a regional workshop with participation across stakeholder groups and explore whether their effort would be accepted as consistent with regional and community hopes. The workshop was framed as an effort to build local economies. In choosing a sufficiently broad and noncontroversial topic, Frank and Christine hoped to minimize the possibility of distracting arguments about the future of mining. The workshop would explore the issue of local economies, but it would also answer the question of whether an intervention would actually be welcomed.

On September 28, 2010, approximately sixty people gathered at the University of Virginia's College at Wise for a workshop titled Building Local Economies in Southwest Virginia. Frank and Christine convened and facilitated the meeting. Participants' thoughts were solicited throughout the meeting to help determine interest in the projects and inform possible next steps.

The meeting began with three presentations by organizations working at the regional scale in the area. The presentations both informed attendees

FIGURE 5.2 A stakeholder meeting of the Clinch River Valley initiative.
E. Franklin Dukes.

of efforts in the region and allowed individuals representing diverse and, in some instances, conflicting interests to sit in the same space without confrontation. After these presentations, the group discussed needs and opportunities for local food systems, green building and low-income housing, and downtown revitalization and artisan networks, all topics that had been suggested during stakeholder interviews.

The second part of the meeting focused on the Spearhead Trail of the Southwest Regional Recreation Authority, a new entity that was hoping to make a mark in the region. This discussion provided opportunities for people who are working on different efforts to connect with one another. Participants were able to discuss possible concerns and potential funding opportunities. The meeting concluded with dinner and a presentation and discussion with two guests from Oregon who shared their experiences with the transition from a natural-resource-based economy (in that case, timber) to a more diversified economy.

Judging from workshop evaluations and comments made at the end of the session, the September 2010 meeting was an overwhelming success. One participant deemed it the most inclusive and effective meeting he could recall. While noting that a good deal of collaboration already occurs in the region, participants believed that this meeting was distinguished by the diversity of participants and the sense that people with conflicting views could nonetheless find common ground (see boxes on Lou Ann Wallace and Shannon Blevins, below).

The following morning, a small planning meeting with about a dozen regional leaders, most of whom had participated in the previous day's meeting, was held to discuss possible next steps. Participants agreed that four areas of focus attracted the most interest: (1) facilitating discussions for downtown planning and access for all-terrain vehicles; (2) planning for building local food systems; (3) engaging in targeted community capacity building, particularly around facilitation; (4) continuing the regional, cross-sector convening on building local economies.

CONDUCTING THE PROCESS

Over the next six months, Frank, Christine, and their IEN colleagues continued to assess how best to proceed. While their assessment, preparatory work, and initial meetings had legitimized their entry into the coalfields, much remained to be done for them to be able to say that they had an authentic consensus-building project. The only funding was an initial, small grant from Virginia's Department of Forestry; they had no leadership group from the region, such as a steering committee, to provide guidance and local legitimacy; no additional meetings had been scheduled; the project scope was still very general; and, despite the enthusiasm expressed at the initial meetings, they had no guarantee that this enthusiasm would lead to a sustained effort.

They prepared a project statement listing several components that might appeal to potential funders.[4] Over the next several months, they organized and convened a second meeting that focused on identifying potential goals and opportunities, information needs and gaps, additional participants, and next steps for the strategic planning process.

On February 9, 2011, fifty-four people gathered at the Oxbow Center in St. Paul, Virginia. Again, this meeting attracted a diverse group of people with environmental, economic, and social interests. When invited to describe their interests as part of introducing themselves, participants expressed a wide range of goals.[5] During the workshop, stakeholders used a combination of presentations about current activities and small-group breakout sessions to refine goals. The more refined goals included a focus on water quality and environmental protection for the Clinch River; support for entrepreneurs, particularly those who might promote recreation; and improving the infra-structure for tourism. A new goal that emerged from this meeting—one that seemed to reflect a developing consensus vision—was to establish a state park that would attract tourists and support entrepreneurial businesses, pro-vide recreational opportunities, and protect the water quality and the world-class biodiversity of the Clinch River. Participants enthusiastically agreed to meet again, this time sooner rather than later, to develop a plan that would bring these goals into being. In the interim Frank and Christine's project team assessed meeting results and consulted with stakeholders.

On May 11, 2011, project participants met again in St. Paul to fur-ther develop a strategy for integrating economic development and envi-ronmental protection.[6] The largest meeting to date, some seventy-seven stakeholders refined goals and actions to meet those goals.[7] Although concerns about encouraging youth to stay in the region dominate any discussion of the coalfields' future, few initiatives engage young people directly. For the first time in this effort, there was an explicit youth component. A panel discussion, Creating a Vision for the Future of the Clinch River Watershed, featured local students from St. Paul High

School. Panel and meeting participants discussed their concerns, ideas, and vision for the Clinch River watershed.

This large group developed four preliminary goal areas. Participants then broke into four small groups consistent with these goals:

Group 1: exploring a possible Clinch River State Park (and feasibility study for the park)

Group 2: developing and integrating access points, trails, and campgrounds along the Clinch River

Group 3: exploring environmental education and water quality enhancement opportunities in the Clinch River watershed

Group 4: connecting outdoor recreation and downtown revitalization; fostering entrepreneurship and marketing strategies

After the small-group discussions, participants reconvened to discuss the ideas and priorities around each goal area. Finally, action groups formed to continue working on the goal areas. Group 3 decided that its goals were too broad and that environmental education and water quality required separate sets of actions. At this meeting, stakeholders again agreed to convene another time, in late summer.

CONTINUING AND EXPANDING THE PROCESS

CRVI began as an informal, occasional gathering of stakeholders with diverse interests who were exploring possible shared interests. Even though Frank and Christine were closely engaged in the activities, they cannot say with certainty when this exploration transitioned into a branded initiative within a fixed region (Russell, Scott, Tazewell and, Wise Counties and the towns within), with expectations among stakeholders for continuity and expansion. But by summer of 2011, this transition was evident. Participants were asking for more meetings and bringing up the need for funding. Some were not waiting for confirmed plans to undertake concrete short-term actions, such as providing new access points for canoeing and kayaking on the Clinch River.

At the next planned meeting, in August 2011, participants developed a draft vision for the Clinch River Action Plan, presented action group updates, and then met in small groups to refine and plan next steps for each goal. At the end of the meeting, each group reported out on their next steps. The enthusiasm and energy demonstrated that the participants in these meetings now identified as a group with shared goals.

Perhaps most significant in the transition from an ad hoc gathering organized by Frank, Christine, and their IEN colleagues to a sustained initiative led primarily by stakeholders themselves, several participants agreed to serve on a steering committee to guide the planning effort. Steering committee members agreed to draft a vision statement incorporating the ideas generated to date. And participants endorsed a name for the project: the Clinch River Valley Initiative.

By the next meeting, in October 2011, the draft vision had been finalized and the structure of CRVI clarified. That vision reaches high: "By 2020, the Clinch River Valley will be a global destination based on its unique biodiversity, natural beauty, cultural attractions and outdoor opportunities. This collaboration will bring measurable economic, environmental and social benefits to the region's communities while protecting the Clinch's globally rare species."

Five goals, each with an active action group, also were finalized:

Goal 1: Develop a Clinch River State Park.

Goal 2: Develop and integrate access points, trails, and campgrounds along the Clinch River.

Goal 3: Enhance water quality in the Clinch River.

Goal 4: Develop and enhance environmental education opportunities for all community members in the Clinch River watershed.

Goal 5: Connect and Expand Downtown Revitalization, Marketing and Entrepreneurial Development Opportunities in the Clinch River Valley.

Why is it that some collaborative processes attempt change and fail, while others attempt change and succeed? This question has been a subject of much research (see, e.g., Dukes, Firehock, and Birkhoff 2011), and some elements of a successful process are easy to observe: strong local leadership, as demonstrated by chairs and participants in the action groups; a clear need and shared purpose; resources to support the effort; and effective facilitation and coordination.

Some elements are tied more to intangibles or to the personalities and motivations of the people who become involved. Two of CRVI's many leaders are profiled in the accompanying boxes.

Lou Ann Wallace

Lou Ann Wallace introduces herself by saying, "I'm just a regular person," and eventually even claiming that she is "just a nobody." She then quickly demonstrates why these are the only statements she gets wrong as she shares her long history of citizen involvement. A communication business she founded, with customers such as Morton Salt, the College of William and Mary, and various coal companies, allowed her to work at home and to have some time for civic affairs.

When she first became an elected town councillor in the mid-1990s, she would return home in the evening frustrated with her fellow councillors. They would spend months talking about putting a roof on the fire hall while her town of St. Paul, with some one thousand residents, was losing its businesses, its young people, and its identity.

She eventually found other neighbors who shared her concerns and who, like her, wanted to live in St. Paul and to raise a family there. She credits Bill Kitrell of the Nature Conservancy with responding to her near-desperate plea for help in securing a small grant to begin a visioning effort. She and those neighbors undertook the visioning exercise and developed a strategic plan for the town of St. Paul to accompany a powerful, comprehensive vision that incorporates economy, education, culture, and stewardship of the environment. Thanks to their strategy, they have created some thirty-one miles of trails, a farmers' market, and, more important, a new identity for St. Paul.

Wallace eventually began paying more attention to the environment; for instance, she learned that a wetlands property she and her husband had purchased was less a mosquito-breeding area than a valuable addition to the homestead. This interest led her to being elected to the county's soil and water conservation board, becoming the president of the statewide association of such boards, and eventually earning a gubernatorial appointment on Virginia's State Water Control Board, the regulatory authority for the Department of Environmental Quality.

She has learned that to get things done she can go through the front door, but when the front door is closed she can find a way through the back door. And when the back door doesn't work, she and her partners do it themselves—letter writing, refinishing floors, or whatever it takes. She describes how they wanted healthier food and started the local farmers' market with no funding at all. She has a world-class vision: a "champagne vision on a beer budget," as she phrases it. In four years that market grew from a tent—and the need to call her neighbors to badger them into buying the produce—to a permanent structure and a venture that makes good money for the vendors. She is an active leader in CRVI, recruiting members for the action groups and making valuable connections among local residents and state organizations.

Shannon Blevins

Shannon Blevins is director of economic development for the University of Virginia's College at Wise. She spent twelve years in private business, primarily working with call centers. She is candid about the challenges in health, education, and workforce preparedness in the region. Her quiet demeanor belies the determination and energy she brings to that role, along with a recognition that her work requires a long-term investment of time and attention.

She sees her work as changing the paradigm of economic development. Success will not come from recruitment of big-box industries but from the ability to innovate and build on what is already in the region.

This approach characterizes what is now called the Appalachian Prosperity Project. APP consists of the Virginia Coalfield Coalition, made up of the two regional planning district commissions (seven counties, one city, and one town) for southwestern Virginia, the University of Virginia, and the University of Virginia's College at Wise. As she is quick to note, the ideas come from the grass roots; the APP does not exert control but instead supports local individuals and communities by taking on such tasks as scheduling meetings, taking notes, and providing a location.

Many people used to work in silos; the new paradigm necessitates reaching across boundaries and working with new and unfamiliar partners. The new paradigm recognizes that health, education, and entrepreneurship are keys to a strong economy. Blevins is pleased that the Clinch River Valley Initiative incorporates all three of those elements and more at the same time. Outdoor recreation offers wonderful opportunities to be outside, and the same is true for environmental education—with the potential for bringing in people from around the world to study the unique biodiversity of the river. And there is a lot of opportunity for residents of the region to develop businesses with the river at their core.

This chapter's opening vignette displays how vibrant CRVI has become and how the role of the IEN project team, led by Frank and Christine, has shifted. The vision of CRVI members is driving the activities, and momentum continues to build. Stakeholders are excited about the future, and people in nearby areas are asking if their region might begin a similar effort.

CRVI represents everything stakeholders are interested in: local assets; seven towns undertaking downtown revitalization; a strong, positive regional identity. It is a model for other communities. Todd Christensen, profiled earlier, describes this as the first time in his thirty years in government that he has seen diverse government agencies working together so well. He credits that to the reality that no single agency or group is in charge, and that an honest broker not affiliated with any agency is facilitating the collaborative work.

As this book goes to press, funds are being raised and planning continues. CRVI is mentioned in local government meetings, and questions are no longer raised about "Should we have a state park?" or "Should we increase access to the river?" but rather people ask "Where should we put the state park?" and "Where should the access points go?" At the December 2013 meeting of Shaping Our Appalachian Region (SOAR) conference in Pikeville, Kentucky, CRVI was featured as a model of regional cooperation.

The CRVI steering committee is grappling with the question of project sustainability. Should CRVI incorporate? Might it lose any of the spirit of collaboration if it were to do so? Although the future is always uncertain, CRVI is in a good place. Group members are not wondering when success might come but how to maintain and build on that success.

SIX

Stakeholders and the Politics of Conflict

*In the fall of 2010, Washington, DC, witnessed several competing appeals to demo-
cratic values made by individuals involved in the conflict over MTM. During a pro-
mining rally in mid-September, billed as Stand Up for American Coal Jobs, miners
and supporters of mining massed at Union Station, a major transportation hub and
tourist destination in the nation's capital, where they shared their message with thousands of commuters. Four hundred of these pro-mining activists marched to Capitol
Hill to hear endorsements of their cause from pro-coal politicians. They demanded
that Congress support MTM and other forms of mining. Signs at the rally in support
of coal read Coal Miners Love Mountains Too. Virginia Senator Mark Warner, a
Democrat, told the cheering crowd, "No one should be making the rules who hasn't
been underground" (NMA 2010).*

*Barely a week later, hundreds of people from Appalachia, the southeast, and
across the country gathered at a weekend workshop at Georgetown University called
Appalachia Rising (see Appalachia Rising 2010). This event brought together a variety of advocacy and activist groups working against MTM and supporting local
communities and the preservation of the mountains. Vowing that "Appalachians are
not and never will be collateral damage," one of the organizers reminded the audience
that "we all breathe the same air and drink the same water and the justice we want for
our community is the same justice we want for all communities who are facing oppres-
sion and exploitation." On the following Monday, many Appalachia Rising attendees
rallied near the White House. Over one hundred were arrested while engaging in
nonviolent civil disobedience against MTM.*

The fall 2010 activities were among the largest related to MTM that had
ever taken place in Washington, DC. They vividly displayed the strategy that
had evolved for some Appalachian stakeholders in the conflict: stakeholders for and against MTM were seeking to express their views to the federal
government and to the broader public. In their efforts, anti-MTM interests
urged the Obama administration to enforce surface-mining regulations protective of public health and of environmental quality. They also demanded that

Congress outlaw the practice of MTM entirely. For their part, pro-mining interests wanted the administration to interpret regulations in the same ways
they had been during the Bush administration, when MTM was thriving, and
to embrace coal as part of the plan to meet the nation's energy needs.

Along with the shift of focus to Congress, the president, and the federal
agencies came increased use of the media to promote the issues and to expose
and criticize those who held opposing points of view. In part these efforts
were designed to raise consciousness among a population—in the region
and the nation—that may be largely unaware of the MTM conflict and yet
reliant on energy from the burning of coal mined using MTM. These dem-
onstrations were evidence of the commitment of those living and working
in the coalfields to increase their activism outside Appalachia and to reach
a broader public with their concerns. For stakeholders on all sides of the
conflict, the heated controversy over the future of MTM and of coal generally was one facet of a broader struggle over the energy future of the United
States. This struggle often pits advocates for coal against those promoting
energy conservation and energy alternatives, including not only renewables
such as solar and wind power but, increasingly, nonrenewable natural gas.

This chapter explores the parallel efforts by stakeholders in the MTM
conflict to gain public awareness and support for their views of MTM in
order to influence elected officials and change national policy. In the past,
anti-MTM activists had relied on the support of national environmental
organizations to lobby at the federal level for policy changes. More recently,
they also had been coming in increasing numbers for a Day of Action once
or twice each year to speak directly with politicians. The coal industry and
the unions always had lobbyists who communicated with elected federal officials on their behalf. Nevertheless, they felt a need to expand their efforts
in response to the increasing support that the anti-MTM activists were re-
ceiving from the general public and to regulatory decisions that threatened
their mining practices. Thus, developments in the conflict and in the US
political climate led these stakeholders to change their strategy. As the late
anti-MTM activist Judy Bonds told one of the authors in June 2010, "This is
our civil rights moment. It's time for us to march on Washington."

The following two sections explain why action at the level of the federal government became increasingly important for a large number of

stakeholders and how escalating the conflict to the highest level of political decision making affected stakeholder relationships and interests. The fall 2010 activities described above were evidence that several stakeholder groups were also trying to influence policy by, among other tactics, increasing the number of people who considered themselves stakeholders in the MTM conflict. A later section chronicles some of the twists and turns in the conflict that emerged as stakeholders sought to increase their numbers and to achieve a more powerful impact through the media during a time of extremely partisan politics. But as attention to MTM grew at the national level, and as the lives of some stakeholders changed, the conflict continued to play out in the coalfields region.

National Politics and the Dynamics of Change

Since the 1970s the federal government has played an important role in regulating MTM and other forms of mining. The Clean Water Act of 1972 (CWA) and its amendments, the Surface Mining Control and Reclamation Act of 1977 (SMCRA), and the other laws that provide the regulatory framework for the mining industry have been at the center of concern and contestation for those who oppose MTM and have been used by the coal industry to defend their pursuits of mining.

As discussed in chapter 4, many people across Appalachia were concerned about the fate of Nationwide Permit 21 (NWP 21), which streamlined the way the Army Corps of Engineers issued permits for MTM. In this instance, and in others that affected MTM, consequential decisions lay within the purview of federal agencies. The description below of two of these instances shows that decisions made at the highest levels of government have consequences for stakeholders at lower levels and that political partisanship, the political process, and goals linked to a particular administration can shape decisions and stakeholder behavior. The political climate in which agencies make decisions—whether a time of bipartisan collaboration or of staunch party-line voting—influences administrative decision making. Consequently, as the two examples suggest, decisions at the federal level can have wide-ranging effects on stakeholders at all levels as well as on the practice of coal mining.

DEFINING *FILL*

The conflict over MTM is influenced by the decisions of many individuals and organizations. One very small decision led to a significant opportunity to expand MTM. In 2002 the EPA and the Army Corps of Engineers made an agreement that redefined one word in the Clean Water Act (CWA). That word was *fill*.

In what was to become a strange odyssey, the Army Corps began granting permits in the 1980s for mining overburden to be placed in valleys adjacent to mining sites. The section of the CWA that guided the Army Corps (Section 404) specifically mentioned fill material, but did not define *fill*. Court challenges followed swiftly, and many allegations invoked the CWA's prohibition on placing waste in streams. A 1999 federal-court decision often referred to as *"Bragg"* challenged the Army Corps's permitting practices, and the mining industry reeled under the prospect of a virtual shutdown of MTM operations (*Bragg v. Robertson* 1999).

In a settlement related to *Bragg,* the Clinton administration agreed to develop a comprehensive approach to awarding permits that would clarify how the regulations would apply and thus reduce the potential for lawsuits. One concern that the EPA addressed during President Clinton's administration was the legal fighting over how the term *fill* was understood by the EPA and the Army Corps, as those two agencies had interpreted *fill* in completely different ways.[1] Also at play were rising political stakes in advance of the 2000 presidential election, including the attention paid by candidate George W. Bush to coal counties in southern West Virginia and the concerns raised by industry about what an Al Gore presidency might mean for federal environmental regulation. Yet before the competing visions of *fill* could be reconciled, a higher court set aside the *Bragg* decision, and the harmonizing discussions faltered.

After President Bush took office in 2001, J. Steven Griles, deputy secretary at the Department of the Interior who had previously worked as a coal industry lobbyist, made the following promise to the West Virginia Coal Association:"We will fix the federal rules very soon on water and spoil placement" (Warrick 2004). Not long afterward, the Bush administration finished the job of redefining *fill* that Clinton had started. *Fill* was defined to *include* "overburden, slurry, or tailings or similar mining-related materials." Only "trash and garbage" were excluded as fill under Section 404, and consequently a wide range of material could be placed in streams.[2] Journalist Michael Shnayerson describes these changes in his book *Coal River*: "On May 3, 2002, the new definition was finished and made public. Fill, the administration declared, need not be defined as having a primary purpose of filling a streambed or wetlands for construction. Almost anything that had that *effect* was fill. With this seemingly minor change, the whole law was turned on its head" (Shnayerson 2008, 122, emphasis in original). Defining one small word meant that almost anything, including mining waste, could be placed in streams, and this administrative act unleashed new rounds of permitting for surface mines.[3]

Many commentators emphasize the highly political nature of this rule change. Sam Evans (2010) suggests that the EPA and the Army Corps under the Bush administration might have been victims of "agency capture," whereby powerful stakeholders from outside the government in fact control agency actions. This serious accusation could be understood to involve abuse of political authority and cynical manipulation of the law for political and economic gain (Drew and Oppel 2009).[4] Although employment protections for federal employees charged with developing and implementing federal regulations allow for some independence, career employees are managed by political appointees who share the goals of, and are dependent for their jobs on, whichever administration is in power.[5] From their perspective, industry leaders and other powerful stakeholders were seeking to achieve clarity in the regulations so that they could proceed with mining projects.

However, this clarity was to be short-lived. In early 2010 Lisa Jackson, the EPA administrator under President Barack Obama, commented that her agency was looking into the possibility of new rules about fill (Dickinson 2010). As described below, several subsequent EPA actions had significant impacts on MTM; these actions also were depicted as highly politicized.

THE SPRUCE MINE VETO

After President Obama took office, environmental protection agencies at the federal and state levels began to review mining permits that had been granted by the Army Corps of Engineers. One review raised questions about the permits to dispose of mining waste from Spruce No. 1 Mine, owned by Mingo Logan Coal Company and located near Charleston, West Virginia, in the Coal River basin. The permit for Spruce No. 1 Mine had been requested in 1997 and granted in 2007 by the Corps. In March 2010 the EPA proposed that the permit be revoked unless the company significantly revised its plan for mining and valley fills. The EPA's proposal was followed by a comment period during which many stakeholders weighed in. In May 2010, 121 comments were made at a public hearing held near the proposed mine site. Although tensions were high among the attendees, who numbered over five hundred, no violence broke out. While 65 percent of the comments at the hearing opposed the EPA's proposed action, 70 percent of the fifty thousand written comments sent to the EPA supported its proposal to revoke the permit (EPA 2011c).

Stakeholders on all sides of the MTM conflict were well aware of the Spruce No. 1 controversy when they gathered in Washington, DC, in the fall of 2010 for the activities mentioned at the outset of this chapter. The EPA would likely issue its final determination about Spruce No. 1 in the coming months. If Spruce No. 1 were to go forward, over six miles of streams in the Coal River basin would be covered over by valley fills. Yet to stop that from happening, the EPA would have to take the unprecedented action of revoking a permit that had already been granted.

In January 2011 the EPA did in fact revoke the permit, issuing a ninety-nine-page report (EPA 2011c) to justify its decision. The EPA based the decision on many factors but highlighted scientific studies of the mine's negative environmental impact on the region. These studies posited that mining Spruce No. 1 Mine as proposed would result in harmful effects to the environment, including high conductivity levels in surrounding water bodies and threats to insects, fish, and wildlife.[6]

A press release indicated that the EPA's unprecedented decision could have been avoided:

> EPA's final determination on the Spruce Mine comes after discussions with the company spanning more than a year failed to produce an agreement that would lead to a significant decrease in impacts to the environment and Appalachian communities. The action prevents the mine from disposing the waste into streams unless the company identifies an alternative mining design that would avoid irreversible damage to water quality and meets the requirements of the law. Despite EPA's willingness to consider alternatives, Mingo Logan did not offer any new proposed mining configurations. (EPA 2011b)

The EPA justified its opposition to the mining plans not only through the environmental impact studies that had been conducted but also out of concern that the proposed valley fills would destroy cultural resources that the federal agency is charged to protect (see box on environmental justice).

Environmental Justice

The phrase *environmental justice* has multiple meanings yet is becoming an increasingly important term in environmental conflict. Environmental justice is also playing an increasing role in the MTM conflict and is used in arguments for and against MTM. Several of the anti-MTM groups identify environmental justice as central to their approach (Hufford 2003; Morrone and Buckley 2011; Shapiro 2010). The EPA justified its ruling on the Spruce No. 1 Mine permit in part by arguing that the effects of the mine and valley fills would not be in keeping with the agency's mandate to strive for environmental justice. Executive Order 12898 directs the EPA and other federal agencies to make the achievement of environmental justice "part of its mission by identifying and addressing, as appropriate, disproportionately high and adverse human health or environmental effects of its programs, policies, and activities on minority populations and low-income populations." It was the EPA's determination that the proposed Spruce No. 1 Mine valley fills would adversely impact a small, very-low-income community and would also have a negative cultural impact by making it impossible for residents to use the common mountain ridges where they hunted, fished, and gathered local herbs (EPA 2011c). Concerns over whether the local population had been adequately consulted about their perspective on the mine were also relevant to the EPA, as the agency must seek "the fair treatment and meaningful involvement of all people regardless of race, color, national origin, or income with respect to the development, implementation, and enforcement of environmental laws, regulations, and policies" (EPA 2011c, 94).

Those who opposed the EPA's stance on Spruce No. 1 Mine took a different approach to environmental justice, as articulated by Terry Headley, a public relations consultant for the West Virginia Coal Association:

> Entire communities that depend on mining will be put at risk—their lifeblood, the revenues generated by coal, will vanish with the industry, leaving ghost towns across the region. This is not an exaggeration! These are very real fears.
>
> And just as individual communities and our industry vanish, so will roughly 20 percent of the state's economic base, creating poverty and an exodus from West Virginia that will make the Dust Bowl and the Great Depression pale in comparison.
>
> We hear a great deal of talk coming from Washington about "economic justice" and "environmental justice." There is NOTHING JUST about your action! There is NOTHING FAIR about your action! (Headley 2010, emphasis in original)

With support from the coal industry and the unions, Mingo Logan Coal Company had already been seeking to block the EPA's action through the legal system. Once the decision was final, they redoubled their efforts in court, and pro-coal interests spoke out strongly against the EPA and the Obama administration.

The high-stakes decision on Spruce No. 1 Mine was undertaken during a very contentious period of US politics.[7] The summer and fall of 2010 was a time of fierce partisan fighting over numerous issues, as Republican groups, especially the Tea Party movement, railed against many of the policies proposed by President Obama and the federal agencies working under his administration. Shortly after the president's inauguration, Senator Mitch McConnell, from the coal-producing state of Kentucky, vowed to work against Obama's reelection and was among the first politicians to charge the president with waging a "war on coal" (cf. Ward 2012d). On most issues, party affiliation dictated whether a politician would support the president's view, with Republicans in opposition and Democrats in support. However, Democratic politicians with roots in coal states, such as Governor (later Senator) Joe Manchin in West Virginia, crossed party lines to speak out against the administration's approach to coal, as did Senator Jay Rockefeller from West Virginia.

After the election of a Republican majority in the House of Representatives in 2010, the EPA's actions were even more highly scrutinized, with threatened budget consequences for policies or actions deemed unfavorable to powerful stakeholders. In early 2011 one House budget proposal recommended completely defunding the EPA. As the Spruce No. 1 Mine issue made its way into the courts yet again, the new Congress began in January 2011 to organize to rein in what some members viewed as gross overreach by the EPA.[8]

In the redefinition of *fill* and the EPA's veto of the Spruce No. 1 Mine permit, powerful stakeholders, including politicians, were influential in administrative rulings at the federal level that subsequently had significant effects on stakeholders at all levels. For the most part, major changes in regulations can be difficult to achieve. Stakeholders might advocate for a position for years without the EPA or another agency paying much attention. But in some instances, a shift in the administration or Congress can result in a 180-degree turn on an issue, such as a new definition of *fill* or the Obama administration's emphasis on using scientific evidence to determine clean-water policy. Getting caught in partisan political struggles can be disheartening for those stakeholders who lack the money, power, or influence to play a role in determining the outcomes of battles fought, won, and refought on politicized landscapes far from their own spheres of influence.

Stakeholder Participation at the Federal Level

The controversy over Spruce No. 1 Mine, and the subsequent push-back by pro-MTM interests and politicians, brought stakeholders from the coalfields region to the federal arena in greater numbers than ever. Many stakeholders had hoped that their issue would reach that venue, but once there, did they get what they wanted? What can the stakeholders who usually focus their activities in local areas expect, when the conflict shifts more to the national level?

For those stakeholders who are positioned on the front lines of the MTM conflict, appealing to the federal government poses difficulties. Traveling to Washington, DC, to protest or to speak with an official is not nearly as easy or familiar as engaging in such actions at the state capital or even more locally. Communicating with federal officials is complicated, too, as they are often shielded from stakeholders, especially any who might criticize their position. The political culture of the nation's capital can be a significant barrier; powerful stakeholders who are familiar with federal policy making (e.g., industry and finance executives or national environmental organizations) generally have an advantage of access over ordinary citizens. Finally, stakeholders who want to address regulatory issues need to understand the technical discourses of science and law. When lawyers, scientists, policy wonks, and lobbyists become prominent actors in increasing numbers, locally based activists might find their own efforts eclipsed or sidelined, and stakeholder groups can experience internal tension.

A CONGRESSIONAL HEARING FROM A STAKEHOLDER PERSPECTIVE

The following description of a congressional subcommittee hearing held in May 2011 provides a glimpse of how groups of locally active stakeholders experienced the federal government. The title of the hearing, EPA's

Mining Policy: Assault on Appalachian Jobs, makes clear the pro-mining perspective taken by the congressional representatives who initiated it. Calling a hearing allows members of Congress to demonstrate to stakeholders—whether constituents, lobbyists, or industry representatives—that they are "doing something" about an issue. By asking pointed questions, they can also subject witnesses to public praise or criticism and thus score political points with certain key stakeholders. Finally, since Congress has to approve budgets for all federal agencies and programs, members may use that power to attempt to influence agency behavior.

Long before the hearing began, anti-MTM activists began assembling in a large hallway of the Rayburn House Office Building. At the front of the line were environmental activists from major organizations based in Washington, DC, as well as local Appalachian groups, such as Coal River Mountain Watch. A few wore T-shirts that read Save the Endangered Hillbilly, and many in line sported I ♥ Mountains buttons. Not long before the doors opened, about twenty-five people wearing white T-shirts with the pro-coal FACES of Coal logo joined the line at the back. With the seats for observers and the press entirely filled, the committee chair opened the proceedings and invited panelists to speak. The four men who spoke all supported the coal industry.[9] A previous hearing held in March had similarly included only opponents of the administration's policy. The majority of questions from committee members were designed to allow them to present very negative views of the EPA.

Not surprisingly, a hearing in a divided Congress would present a strong opposition to administration policy. Opponents of MTM sitting in the audience shouted out a few questions for the panel. When the committee chair admonished them to be quiet, several covered their mouths with duct tape, while others tried to shame committee members for silencing the anti-MTM perspective. Eventually, as security personnel moved into the audience, a few of the most prominent protestors left.

A second period of questioning included only one panelist: Nancy Stoner, the EPA's Acting Assistant Administrator in the Office of Water. Most of the questions put to her by the committee challenged the EPA's recent actions around mining. Her answers reflected one basic point: the EPA was mandated to protect the health of people and the environment.

When challenged that she should also be concerned about economic consequences for the communities affected, Stoner held her ground. Under tough questioning, she insisted repeatedly that the EPA evaluates the health and safety issues of proposed mining and does so by looking at scientific evidence. She pointed to numerous scientific studies that confirmed the negative consequences of valley fills for health and environment. Committee members, especially those from coal states, made points about the EPA's overreach and the negative effects of its actions on business and on energy security. Stoner and the committee members talked past each other, as they articulated very different understandings of the priorities at stake.

During Stoner's testimony, audience members were engaged but more subdued. Those wearing FACES of Coal T-shirts frowned in disapproval at some of Stoner's answers and were cheered by critical comments from committee members. The anti-MTM attendees smiled in support of Stoner and nodded vigorously when she made a point favorable to their perspective.

Stoner, an EPA administrator, is also a stakeholder, as she is expected to act on behalf of the public. Her understanding of the public's interests is, thus, consequential. The committee members represented diverse positions as stakeholders, with those from coal states expressing urgency about the issue. But the description of the hearing shows that it can also be very difficult for less powerful stakeholders to believe that they are being heard or that their position is even recognized.

Federal-level attention to a conflict brings the promise of a major payoff, but, returning to the issues raised earlier, it can mean that powerful and influential stakeholders are those most actively involved in decision making. At the same time, those stakeholders who care deeply, but have little influence, might find themselves unable to participate effectively. Depending on their position, some stakeholders might be drawn into the political arena for the first time, as was likely the case for some pro-coal attendees at the hearing who looked pleased at the tough questions asked by the representatives from the coal states.

About a month later, several of the anti-MTM stakeholders who had been silenced during the subcommittee hearing expressed themselves loudly at a rally outside EPA headquarters in Washington, DC. They wanted to draw attention to the MTM issue and to support the EPA for its efforts to protect Appalachia from MTM's negative impact. With music and rousing speeches directed to EPA employees passing by and looking down at the rally from their office windows, stakeholders sought to make a human connection with the people whose work they valued. Only a few media outlets covered the small rally of about thirty people. Attendees noted that many other people wanted to attend but could not, because they were involved in a major anti-MTM action called the March on Blair Mountain (see box titled "The Battle of Blair Mountain" in chapter 2).

Cultivating New Stakeholders

Rallies, tree sits (where individuals create a human "nest" high in a tree, in this case near or on a mining site, and resist removal), congressional hearings, public meetings, and many other activities are designed to raise awareness of the conflict over MTM, which means cultivating new stakeholders by reaching out to people who do not even perceive themselves as stakeholders. When little attention was being paid to the expansion of MTM, local activists began to raise awareness among politicians and ordinary people who might be sympathetic. At times when limitations on mining seemed likely, pro-coal activists, particularly industry lobbyists, reached out to gain supporters.

This section of the chapter focuses on stakeholders' efforts to get others involved by enlarging the circle of stakeholders, in effect, convincing more people that they have a stake in the conflict. Their strategies are typically entirely partisan, in the sense of representing just one perspective on the conflict. This narrow way of engaging stakeholders can exacerbate the potential for anger and violence, obscure broader issues at stake, and make creative solutions or compromise appear impossible. But it does enable groups to present their position clearly, albeit in an either-or frame.

Stakeholders on all sides of the issue have turned to the media for coverage of their activities and promotion of their message. Ken Ward Jr.'s articles and blogs in the *Charleston (WV) Gazette* have paid the most consistent attention to MTM issues (see box on Ken Ward Jr.).

Ken Ward Jr.

With roots in West Virginia, Kenneth Ward Jr. has covered mining issues for much of his career as a journalist with the *Charleston Gazette*. When Ken joined the paper, in 1991, his colleague Paul Nyden was already investigating surface mining and asking critical questions about the coal industry. As the MTM conflict began to focus on legal issues, such as how mine companies gained permits for surface mines and valley fills, Ken wrote an award-winning series called Mining the Mountains, which exposed instances of state regulators ignoring or breaking federal laws. In consultation with his editors, Ken has always endeavored to illuminate topics hidden from public view. In the late 1990s Ken's strong commitment to providing the public with information led him to investigate scientific studies that were beginning to confirm MTM's negative impact on the environment. When several of those studies were removed from government websites, Ken tracked them down and made them available. Often critical of the coal industry, Ken wonders how coal operators could have profited for so many years while the population of West Virginia remained so poor. At the same time he is very respectful of the work that miners do and indignant at their treatment by the industry and others who would demean or stereotype them. Although Ken's writing has played a key role in making the case against MTM, he has been criticized by some anti-MTM activists, who urge him to take a more aggressive stance on all issues related to coal or the environment.

As a citizen, Ward is alarmed that people increasingly get their news from sources that push an agenda without presenting evidence for their claims or positions. Even organizations that purport to be working for the public interest do not always tell the full story. His concern with one-sided approaches to complex social problems leads Ken to produce accounts that are, in his words, "fair and truthful" and to use those journalistic standards as his guide. From his perspective, journalists have a duty to serve the public interest rather than one side or another.

In 2009, Ken started a blog called *Coal Tattoo* that takes up many issues related to coal in the region (Ward 2012a). Many stakeholders who follow the MTM conflict turn to *Coal Tattoo* for the latest news. Ken's jump into social media was partly in recognition that blogging might be the best way to reach young people. On his mind was a shift in attitudes that he had witnessed. Twenty years ago miners would justify their hard work as a sacrifice that would allow their children to get an education and pursue a career outside the mines. Today, some young residents of mining states are made to feel that they should look solely to the coal industry for work. This perspective might help justify continuing MTM; however, Ken believes that young people deserve to understand their options. Serious, well read, and witty, Ken has played a key role in the MTM conflict in a job that keeps him extremely busy and yet satisfied that he serves the public during difficult times in the place he calls home.

Conventional media based in Appalachia cover mining extensively, although most of the local media outlets tend to take a pro-coal stance and few raise critical questions about MTM. By contrast, the dozen or more documentary films that have been made about the MTM conflict mostly highlight the anti-MTM perspective (see, e.g., Cavanaugh and Wood 2010; Geller 2009; Haney and Rhodes 2011; Stephens and Sprinkle 2013).

Many stakeholder groups use new media, such as websites, blogs, Twitter, and Facebook, to promote their position and organize their actions. The stakeholder role takes on new dimensions when a person can use a single keystroke to "like" one perspective or another and thus advocate as a particular kind of stakeholder. Perhaps the ease with which one can declare allegiance to a cause results in more people imagining themselves as stakeholders. But what level of commitment is to be expected from stakeholders who sign up over the Internet?

As the fight over MTM moved to Congress and the EPA in 2010, the stakes appeared higher than ever, and many stakeholders took a professional approach to the media. Getting national media exposure would allow parties not only to reach more people but, more important, to get the attention of Washington-based politicians and their staff members. The national environmental groups launched several broad initiatives, with the most notable being the Sierra Club's Beyond Coal campaign (see Sierra Club n.d.), which seeks to end MTM and to close coal-fired power plants as part of the transition to an economy fueled by energy sources other than coal.[10] Since 2007, coal industry groups, such as FACES of Coal, have run many regional- and national-level ads in support of coal and mining. In advance of the 2012 presidential election, large billboards proclaimed that, under the current leadership and EPA policies on coal, Appalachia had become "Obama's No Job Zone." Some ads capitalize on the move to so-called clean coal or green coal, which focuses on reducing the harmful emissions created when burning coal. As one consumer-marketing professional observed, "Adding 'clean' to the word 'coal' was a very shrewd move" (Mulkern 2010).

It takes a powerful and wealthy stakeholder, in the form of a national environmental group or an industry lobbying group, to mount a broad media campaign that includes expensive television advertising. But when these entities argue for a particular position on MTM, they generally do so through the voices and images of individual stakeholders. FACES of Coal's ads often include pictures of individual coal industry employees, while residents of mining areas, including former miners, speak out against coal and MTM in Sierra Club ads. These campaigns use individuals because the stories and voices of people who have an individual stake in a conflict provide emotional connections to the intended audience. Seeing the face of someone who stands to lose or gain in a conflict can be powerfully persuasive, especially for people who are uncertain about where they stand on the issues. It is easier for most potential new stakeholders to identify with individuals rather than with organizations, corporations, politicians, or even an abstract cause.

Only rarely does media coverage attempt to speak to everyone's interests in a deeply divided audience. One example was a special report produced by Cable News Network (CNN) correspondent Soledad O'Brien in the summer of 2011, when local residents were engaged in the fight over permits and also organizing for the March on Blair Mountain. O'Brien's prime-time special report gave unprecedented coverage to the MTM issue and endeavored to represent multiple views without taking a perspective

FIGURE 6.1. A mountain view in southern West Virginia.
Susan F. Hirsch.

or side (O'Brien 2011). This was a tall order, and no one seemed satisfied with the result. Anti-MTM activists criticized the report for adopting the familiar jobs-vs.-environment frame for the conflict, an approach that they believe ignores the complexity of the issues involved. And yet, because the March on Blair Mountain figured prominently in the video, some activist groups were torn between welcoming the national exposure and condemning the distortions and stereotyping. The attention given to one mining family put faces to the anguish that people experience when they wait for a decision about permitting to be made in Washington, DC. All sides were interested in national attention, gaining supporters, and swaying politicians. All sides had to agree that the documentary gave the issue national attention. But in the end it is hard to know whether new stakeholders emerged from the broadcast, what positions they took, or whether any politicians were influenced in any way.

The expansion of the MTM conflict to a national stage was inevitable, given the federal government's role in regulating mining and enforcing environmental laws. At the federal level, powerful and wealthy stakeholders can have a significant effect on regulations and policies, as they marshal technical expertise and political influence. Less-powerful stakeholders, including many who operate primarily at local levels, may find it more difficult to navigate the national political bureaucracy, even as the larger venue offers the chance of a broader audience for their perspectives. All stakeholders in the conflict over MTM have faced the challenge of pursuing their goals at a time of severe political partisanship, and this reality likely hardened the positions of many stakeholders, especially politicians.

With additional parties involved in protest, lobbying, litigation, and public relations, the outcomes of the MTM conflict remain unclear. While all sides have gained allies, and considerable media attention, it is possible that they have also lost the ability to develop solutions to these issues by themselves. The costs of prolonging the conflict continue to increase, yet also increasing is the possibility that significant change will come from transformations in the broader energy economy, as the concluding chapter suggests.

SEVEN

Conclusion

The Prospects for Change

In the previous six chapters, we have examined a wide range of stakeholders and their interests, needs, and concerns. The preceding chapters also offered insights into the motivations and actions of diverse stakeholders and a window into how stakeholder behavior is shaped by decisions made outside the Appalachian communities where MTM is practiced. We have encountered stakeholders at the front lines of the conflict, either promoting MTM or battling against it, and also those stakeholders, including third parties, who have tried to shift the debate away from either-or choices and the stark divisions that can flare into violence. At the same time, we have demonstrated that many stakeholders are looking beyond MTM, and even beyond coal itself, to envision and create a future for their communities.

What will the future bring for mountaintop mining? With the advent of more abundant and cheaper natural gas described later in this chapter, domestic demand for coal has diminished and will likely continue to do so. The US Energy Information Administration (EIA 2013, 71) predicts that the share of electricity generated by coal will drop from the 42 percent it had in 2011 to 35 percent in 2040. Most of that shift is from the increase in natural gas—from 24 percent in 2011 to 30 percent in 2040—with renewable energy sources also increasing from 13 percent to 16 percent during that same period.

Actual coal production east of the Mississippi is expected also to decline, from 456 million short tons in 2011 to 396 in 2040 (EIA 2013, 107). Nonetheless, with coal reserves still expected to last for decades, even declining demand is unlikely to diminish the conflicts over coal's extraction.

Neither is the ardor of community and environmental advocates organizing to save mountaintops likely to decrease, nor that of miners, companies, and their allies fighting to continue mining. Certainly, the miners and companies have jobs and economic profitability at stake. And for the community and environmental advocates, their voices, after all—speaking out against powerful interests—have drawn national attention to an issue that politicians and the public might have ignored. These stakeholders have been remarkably persistent in their efforts and commitments.

Conflict scholars have used the concept of *autistic hostility* to describe stakeholders who no longer communicate with one another and are thus caught in a self-reinforcing process that encourages rumors and threats (Pruitt, Rubin, and Kim 2003). Such situations cry out for intervention that would bring the parties together to address their differences productively or at least try to reduce the chance that the lack of communication might lead to direct violence or the trauma of living under threatening conditions. This is challenging work. The Clinch River Valley Initiative (see chapter 5) has taken hundreds of hours for

FIGURE 7.1. The Clinch River.
E. Franklin Dukes.

the facilitation team and the participants themselves to develop the processes that sustain it and that promise continued benefits. Yet despite the challenge of envisioning that parties who have been working to defeat one another may eventually pursue and even find common ground, there are extraordinary examples of communities embroiled in seemingly intractable environmental conflicts where conflicting parties come together, search for, and find constructive solutions for their future (Dukes, Firehock, and Birkhoff 2011). Change is, indeed, possible and can come in many different forms.

In 2012, just a few months after a CNN special aired (see chapter 6), the Appalachian mining region, along with the rest of the nation, was caught in the grip of election-year politics. US energy policy would be a key issue addressed by candidates for president and other offices, and coal would play a role. Along with highly partisan political ads, a new television, radio, print, and Internet campaign had a more positive, if vague, message. Viewers were urged to "Vote 4 Energy" by individual speakers of many different backgrounds and ages, each of whom proclaims, "I Vote 4 Energy" with the justification that the United States needs energy to stimulate the economy and increase employment opportunities. Although the ads resembled those from each side of the MTM conflict in that they profiled individual stakeholders from a diversity of backgrounds, these ads were not about coal at all. In fact, they were sponsored by and in support of oil and natural gas companies that seek a larger role for those fuels in the nation's energy portfolio. A Vote 4 Energy would, in fact, be a vote against coal. These ads were indicative of a development that would have enormous consequences for the MTM conflict: the rise in the importance of oil and natural gas as plentiful domestic fuels.

The first decades of the twenty-first century have seen a new interest in the large concentration of natural gas buried deeply in many parts of Appalachia. Technological innovations allowed for extraction of the gas using hydraulic fracturing, also known as fracking. This innovation, despite the controversies over noise, air, and water pollution that it generates, led many industries, including the largest electrical power companies, to turn away from coal, because burning coal causes more air pollution than burning gas and thus poses additional costs. As fracking expanded rapidly, falling gas prices also accelerated the turn away from coal and the shift in priorities for the energy industry.

The shifting energy outlook—pushed by technological innovation and economic markets as much as concern over the environment—led some stakeholders to change their perspective on the MTM conflict. Two of the coal industry's staunchest and most powerful supporters gave speeches outlining abrupt and remarkable turnabouts.

First was a speech in December 2009 by the longest-serving US senator in history, Robert C. Byrd (D-WV). This speech, in which Byrd admitted that concerns about coal's extraction were legitimate and re-quired action, called for "an open and honest dialogue about coal's future" and was a significant break with the industry line he had been known to promote (Ward 2009b; Ward 2010b). Given that Senator Byrd was only to live a few more months, people could later dismiss his speech as either a deathbed conversion or the product of a confused mind. Others were thrilled that Byrd had finally found the courage to challenge the industry that had long supported him, and that he had defended throughout his political career.

However, on June 20, 2012, Senator Jay Rockefeller (D-WV) made yet another astonishing speech on the floor of the US Senate (Koss and Russell 2012; Ward 2012c). Although his initial entry into politics de-cades before saw him criticizing surface-mining practices, for most of his Senate career Rockefeller had been a very good friend to the coal industry as well as an MTM supporter in his public remarks and posi-tions. Yet his speech attempted to persuade fellow senators to reject a resolution that would condemn the EPA for its efforts to set new air pollution standards for the coal industry. The coal industry badly wanted the resolution passed, and it was breaking news in the coalfields region when Rockefeller spoke in opposition to the resolution and, in effect, in support of EPA regulations.

When Senator Rockefeller spoke out against the coal industry in the summer of 2012, his speech was compared with the one delivered by the late senator Byrd. Yet the biographies of each man provide few clues that would predict their change-of-heart speeches (see box on Byrd and Rockefeller).

Senators Byrd and Rockefeller

A Democrat, Senator Byrd had served over fifty years in the US Congress when he died in office, in June 2010 at the age of ninety-two, just six months after making his remarkable speech about coal. Byrd's early years were spent in poverty in the coalfields of West Virginia, yet he rose to a powerful position as the head of the Senate's Committee on Appropriations. That position enabled Byrd to direct considerable largesse to West Virginia in the form of roads, bridges, and federal facilities, many of which bear his name or the name of a Byrd family member (Byrd 2005; Holley 2010).

Colleagues turned to Byrd as a strong defender of the Constitution and of the Senate's independence. At the same time, in the words of West Virginia Coal Association president Bill Raney, Byrd was "a good friend" to the coal industry for most of his political career (Ward 2010b). The reciprocal relationship between his support for the industry and the industry's support of him at election time perhaps accounts for his initially supportive stance on MTM and most coal-related issues. His speech in December 2010, which called for "an open and honest dialogue about coal's future," was a significant break with the industry (Ward 2009b; Ward 2010b). Part of the honesty he signaled centered on MTM:

> Most people understand that America cannot meet its current energy needs without coal, but there is strong bi-partisan opposition in Congress to the mountaintop removal method of mining it. We have our work cut out for us in finding a prudent and profitable middle ground—but we will not reach it by using fear mongering, grandstanding and outrage as a strategy. As your United States Senator, I must represent the opinions and the best interests of the entire Mountain State, not just those of coal operators and southern coalfield residents who may be strident supporters of mountaintop removal mining. (Byrd 2009)

Jay Rockefeller's relationship with the coal industry was even more complex than Byrd's. He started out his political career in West Virginia in the 1960s by calling for tough regulations over strip mining. But in order to be elected over and over again in a coal state, Rockefeller had to mute his protests and get behind the coal industry. At the end of his political career, he, too, was clear in his denunciation of industry tactics and the hegemony of coal:

> It's not too late for the coal industry to step up and lead by embracing the realities of today and creating a sustainable future. Discard the scare tactics. Stop denying science. Listen to what markets are saying about greenhouse gases and other environmental concerns, to what West Virginians are saying about their water and air, their health, and the cost of caring for seniors and children who are most susceptible to pollution.
>
> Stop and listen to West Virginians—miners and families included—who see that the bitterness of the fight has taken on more importance than any potential solutions. (Rockefeller 2012b; see also Koss and Russell 2012; Ward 2012c)

What explains the change in position expressed by these two politicians? Was it a change of heart for Byrd, a new consciousness as scientific studies began to document the ill effects of MTM on health and environment? Was Rockefeller finally expressing what he had believed all along about surface mining but had dared not admit? Perhaps, for each, their impending plans to leave office allowed them the independence to become statesmen. Or perhaps it was just the right time to say publicly what many had been saying privately. Was it politics—tied inextricably to industry interests—that had kept these leaders from speaking out against the coal industry, despite their personal perspectives? To answer yes to the last question might encourage a deeply cynical view of political leaders and accept that industry had captured the political process. A less cynical analysis would place less emphasis on the role of the coal industry and its lobbyists in calling the shots and more on Byrd and Rockefeller in looking out for West Virginian workers (and voters), who appeared to be largely dependent on a single economic option in the coalfields region. The two explanations are, of course, connected. It is difficult to know for sure what moved these politicians, but these speeches, delivered late in their careers, serve as important examples that change in one's perspective is possible, even when the stakes are high and the stakeholders deeply divided.

Whatever the reasons for his dramatic shift, Rockefeller remained optimistic about the future: "None of this is impossible. Solving big challenges with American ingenuity is what we do. West Virginia knows energy and West Virginia doesn't shrink from challenge. We have the chance here to not just grudgingly accept the future—but to boldly embrace it" (Rockefeller 2012a). Rockefeller, like other politicians before him, was appealing to stakeholders to respond to broad political and economic changes with new perspectives and approaches. His own example, following that of Senator Byrd, illustrates that profound change, expressed publicly, is possible.

Admitting that "coal faces real challenges, even threats," Rockefeller named them: diminishing coal reserves and inefficient coal-fired power plants, the rise of cheap natural gas and the increase in gas-fired power plants, and the general shift to a lower-carbon economy. As this book goes to press, what these and other challenges will mean for MTM and for coal mining is a difficult question on the minds of all stakeholders in the MTM conflict.

If a new economy is built around natural gas, it will likely generate new problems with pollution and labor relations. If the scale of extraction continues to grow unabated, some places might even draw the label of "energy sacrifice zone," which is used increasingly to refer to the Appalachian coalfields (Barry 2012; Morrone and Buckley 2011; Scott 2010). To confront these problems created by gas fracking, will some stakeholders draw on lessons learned in organizing for and against MTM? Will more efforts like the Clinch River Valley Initiative develop? Both scenarios are likely; need stimulates experimentation and success breeds imitation, and throughout the Appalachian coalfields the trend toward communities seeking new ways of sustaining themselves will no doubt continue. The conflict over MTM suggests that changes at the broadest political and economic levels operate in reciprocal relationship with changes in communities and individuals.

We hope that one lesson has been clear: even in situations that might seem to be at a stalemate, stakeholders do in fact have agency to act. In other words, they have an ability to shape how the conflict is expressed and thus to shape the path it takes. As frustrating as the practices of law, policy, and protest may be to stakeholders, they do provide nonviolent options for promoting their views and contesting the perspectives and actions of others. And when stakeholders harness media attention effectively, their influence can be broad and significant. Any call for stakeholders to become involved and to speak out to make others aware of their perspectives must acknowledge the power dynamics that make it hard for certain stakeholders to be heard and to be influential when compared to others. Yet our example shows remarkable shifts in the conflict that occurred through the involvement of a wide range of stakeholders, including local residents who never imagined themselves getting involved. Such shifts can happen quickly: the Clinch River Valley Initiative took less than one year to emerge from initial conception to a sustained, valued effort engaging many dozens of stakeholders who found a place for their vision and energy. This example offers encouragement that the most difficult conflicts might be moved by stakeholders taking action. Participation is, after all, at the base of democratic processes and ideals, and the MTM conflict has demonstrated that individual actions attract attention and change.

If that is the case, how might you, as a reader, consider your role as a stakeholder in the MTM conflict? What might that mean for your actions? Do you take sides with the main protagonists? Do you use the energy from coal-fired power plants without considering the source of that coal? Do you rally against mountaintop mining without considering the potential impact on jobs and livelihoods? Do you work toward a sustainable, prosperous future? If not, are you ready to change?

NOTES

Chapter 2: The Conflict over Mountaintop Mining

1. The website of the organization called I Love Mountains features a program that allows viewers to type in a zip code and trace where the utility that provides their electric power obtains the fuel, often coal, that produces the power (see iLoveMountains n.d.). Power flows from regional and national grids, however, and determining precisely where one's power comes from is thus difficult.

2. This brief section of the chapter offers only an outline of the complex history of coal in Appalachia and points readers toward the many fine histories of coal production in the region (see, e.g., Buckley 2004; Caudill 1963; Eller 2008; Fagge 1996; Gaventa 1980; Lewis 1998; Montrie 2003; Shifflett 1991; Williams 2002). The history of coal in any particular region is connected to coal production and use both nationally and internationally; these histories are beyond the scope of this volume (see, e.g., Freese 2003; Goodell 2006).

3. The notion of "separation" of energy landscapes from other areas is articulated in Black: "Whether a product of zoning, residential preference, or the supply of raw material, most often landscapes of energy production are not seen by most consumers" (2011, 33).

4. Both anthracite and bituminous coal are found in the Appalachian mountain range. Anthracite coal is harder and burns with much less smoke than bituminous coal, which has a higher sulfur content. Attempts to control sulfur emissions into the air have meant that the use of coal for power generation has shifted over the years.

5. Harry M. Caudill's classic book *Night Comes to the Cumberlands* is known less for its sophistication as a work of history than for its success in expressing concern about the region's bleak past and future. Caudill, a West Virginian politician and environmentalist, was the first to declaim the "rape of the Appalachians" in 1962 and thus was at the forefront of the effort to raise awareness about the destructive results of coal mining.

6. According to Timothy Mitchell, "Political possibilities were opened up or narrowed down by different ways of organizing the flow and concentration of energy, and these possibilities were enhanced or limited by arrangements of people, finance, expertise and violence that were assembled in relationship to the distribution and control of energy" (Mitchell 2009, 401; see also Mitchell 2013).

7. On this issue Eller writes, "Mountain politics had always been paternalistic and family-oriented, and when the big coal and timber corporations injected greater economic self-interest into the system, the old ways simply blended with the new political order" (Eller 2008, 33-34). Similarly, the turn to government support in the 1950s drew on and strengthened this "powerful patronage system" (ibid., 34).

8. Michele Morrone and Geoffrey Buckley (2011) note that some critics of environmental injustice in Appalachia have described it as "internal colonialism" that "is no different than the dynamics of global colonial dominance, be it classic imperialism or the corporate capitalist variant of the modern world system" (10–11).

9. There are a variety of types of surface mining, such as open-pit mining, high-wall mining (also called auger mining), strip mining, and others. For descriptions, see, e.g., Freese 2003; IEED 2012; UMWA n.d.

10. The situation was so notorious that John Grisham, author of best-selling legal thrillers, apparently based his novel *The Appeal* on the events (Biskupic 2009).

Chapter 3: Who Is a Stakeholder?

1. According to Roy Lewicki, Barbara Gray, and Michael Elliot, "Framing refers to the process of constructing and representing our interpretations of the world around us. We construct frames by sorting and categorizing our experience—weighing new information against our previous interpretations. . . . When we frame a conflict, we develop interpretations about what the conflict is about, why it is occurring, the motivations of the parties involved, and how the conflict should be settled. And we are likely to frame the conflict differently depending on whether we are an observer of others involved in the conflict, a supporter or an opponent of the disputants, or one of the disputants" (2003, 12).

2. Statistics are disputed; however, there is no question that mining employment has dropped considerably during the period of surface-mining expansion. Former senator Robert Byrd, among many others, argued, "The increased use of mountaintop removal mining means that fewer miners are needed to meet company production goals" (Ward 2009b).

3. For competing perspectives on how the connection between consumers and coalfields is depicted, see http://www.cleancoalusa.org/abundant/where -does-your-electricity-come and http://www.ilovemountains.org/my-connection.

4. Several authors note that John L. Lewis, credited with building the United Mine Workers union, supported both the mechanization of mining, in the 1950s, and also the move to grant firmer legal status to surface mining in the following decades (see Eller 2008; Montrie 2011).

5. This third element comes from the Andrus Family Fund's community reconciliation program; see http://www.affund.org/Community_Reconciliation.html.

6. Robert A. Bush and Joseph P. Folger (1994) are credited with the most popular description of this role in *The Promise of Mediation: Responding to Conflict through Empowerment and Recognition*, in which parties are offered a process of structured communication and care is taken to avoid any hint of such pressure on the disputants.

7. Bargaining is sometimes identified as the subset of negotiation involving only trade-offs, compromise, and other fixed-sum activities.

Chapter 4: Conflict Dynamics and Stakeholder Experiences

1. This issue is articulated in the situation assessment: "At least at the outset, securing effective engagement of the parties may require explicit recognition that the larger struggle about the legitimacy of mountaintop mining will continue to be fought politically, judicially and in the press; it is important that none are being asked to step away from their convictions as a premise for talking with one another" (Adler and Thompson 2008, 25).

2. Owned at the time by the Massey Corporation, Upper Big Branch mine is located above Coal River Road, about twenty miles south of Charleston, West Virginia.

Chapter 5: Building Consensus among Stakeholders

1. http://appalachiantransition.net.

2. In 2010 the focus of one of Frank's graduate classes was the Spearhead Trail, the keystone effort of the Southwest Region Recreational Authority, a

legislature-chartered group in Virginia's coalfields region. Students in the class conducted interviews of key stakeholders and researched how other trails around the country have integrated economic, environmental, and social goals. In 2011 another of Frank's classes was closely integrated with the overall consensus-building process and conducted a broader and more substantial assessment. The 2012 class supported the CRVI effort more directly by examining the possibility of creating a state park.

3. The term *creative economy* has appeared in many places and is often credited to urban planner Richard Florida.

4. Based on the initial assessment and the September 28 meeting, these components included downtown planning with all-terrain vehicle access and outdoor recreational infrastructure needs and a regional collaborative for local food systems planning.

5. The participants' goals are to:

- explore business incubation opportunities and potential partnerships.
- explore how various communities and counties fit into the effort.
- meet project partners and hear others' interests.
- save local assets and focus on enhancing the physical and economic infrastructure of the area as well as increasing marketing efforts.
- take a broad and inclusive approach to the effort, involving multiple stakeholders and agencies and consider the environment and the economy in the planning effort.
- use a consensus-based approach to protect the gem of the Clinch River; use it for revitalization.
- explore opportunities for tying downtown revitalization to Clinch recreation.
- support local, responsible, asset-based development.
- explore ways to add economic value through the river resource.
- involve more citizens and residents in the effort.
- promote tourism in the area's national forests.
- educate and involve students in the effort.

6. On the same day a second meeting was held to ascertain interest in developing a food systems strategy for the region. Previously, graduate students had conducted a food systems assessment of the region to determine how the demand for local food might be met. As this book went to press, the Central Appalachia Food Heritage Project (CAFHP) joins CRVI as a new collaborative, community-based project that envisions a greater understanding

and documentation of regional food heritage to enhance Central Appalachia's regional sustainability and resilience. The CAFHP seeks to build knowledge about heritage place-based foods, and to create future opportunities for economic development and community building in and through our agricultural future. The project is currently housed within the Institute for Environmental Negotiation at the University of Virginia, and builds on the Virginia Food Heritage Project, a similar project taking place in central Virginia. For more on this project, see http://www.vafoodheritage.wordpress.com.

7. They endorsed the need to attract tourists to the region, support entrepreneurial businesses and environmental education, provide recreational opportunities for the region, and protect the water quality and the world-class biodiversity of the Clinch.

Chapter 6: Stakeholders and the Politics of Conflict

1. Section 402 of the CWA allows discharge of waste or pollutant into a water body only if it will not adversely affect water quality. Section 404 operates as an exception to Section 402 to allow for certain materials to be placed into water bodies when necessary for projects such as constructing bridges or dams. The EPA handles permitting for Section 402, and the Army Corps of Engineers regulates Section 404 requests to "discharge dredge and fill" material for projects. Starting in 1977 the Corps used a "purpose-based" approach to Section 404 permits to determine whether something could be discharged as fill. The purpose, usually for a project, had to be to replace water with land or to raise the bottom of a riverbed; the purpose could not be "waste disposal." Any adverse impacts—for instance, on the environment—had to be weighed against the benefits of the proposed purpose (e.g., building a dam). Since the mid-1980s, the EPA has used an "effects-based" approach to Section 402 permits, which focuses on whether the discharge will pollute or degrade the water quality. In general, the EPA gives little weight to benefits and can review any Army Corps decisions, including Section 404 permit decisions. For discussions of the legal controversies over fill, see, for example, Blumm and Zaleha 1989; Browand 2004; Duffy 2002; Evans 2010; Loeb 2007; Shnayerson 2006, 2008.

2. The removal of the general term *waste* from Section 404 permitting was a highly controversial aspect of the change and allowed for anything other than "trash and garbage" to be considered fill.

3. A 2004 *Washington Post* article phrased it similarly: "Today, mountaintop removal is booming again, and the practice of dumping mining debris into

streambeds is explicitly protected, thanks to a small wording change to federal environmental regulations. U.S. officials simply reclassified the debris from objectionable 'waste' to legally acceptable 'fill'" (Warrick 2004, 1).

4. Though unrelated to the controversy over coal, J. Steven Griles was the highest-ranking member of the Bush administration to be imprisoned on corruption charges stemming from the actions of Jack Abramoff, a political lobbyist who was also convicted of corruption. Abramoff was the central figure in multiple scandals involving bribery, money laundering, fraud, and many other charges related to political corruption.

5. If pushed too far, career employees can turn into whistle-blowers. That's what happened to Jack Spadaro, the well-respected head of the National Mine Safety and Health Academy, which is housed in the Department of Labor (House and Howard 2009). When a Bush administration appointee interfered with the report he was writing about the huge coal slurry spill in 2000 in Kentucky, Spadaro spoke out. After publicizing the fact that he and his staff were being held back from investigating violations and negligence by Massey Energy that he believed contributed to the disastrous spill, Spadaro was demoted and endured a variety of forms of retaliation from his supervisors (Leung 2004). He was eventually forced out of the MSHA.

6. Conductivity is a measure of the ability of a given quantity of water to conduct an electric current. Levels of conductivity are proportional to the concentrations of total dissolved solids and major ions in a body of water; some scientists, including a panel of the EPA Science Advisory Board, believe that it is a useful indicator of the influence of runoff in rivers and streams.

7. The lack of bipartisanship was so great that many veteran politicians spoke out in despair against the political climate; several declined to stand for election after 2010, citing the tremendous difficulty of getting anything done in a Congress where political divisions were so deep.

8. In March 2012, a lower court judge reversed the EPA veto, citing that the agency gave itself "stunning power." A three-judge panel on the U.S. Court of Appeals for the D.C. Circuit Court disagreed, thus making clear that the EPA has veto power over permitting decisions, even long after they are granted. In March 2014 the US Supreme Court declined to hear the case, which will likely be considered in a lower court.

9. Michael Carey (Ohio Coal Association), Reed Hopper (Pacific Legal Foundation), Steve Roberts (West Virginia Chamber of Commerce), and Dr. David Sunding (University of California).

10. The Sierra Club gained unfavorable attention when it was revealed that its Beyond Coal campaign was partially funded by up to $26 million from the leadership of Chesapeake Energy, an oil and gas company. The Sierra Club continues to raise awareness about the environmental effects of coal and has since sponsored a Beyond Natural Gas campaign.

REFERENCES

Adler, Peter, and Douglas Thompson. 2008. *Situation Assessment: Mountaintop Mining/ Valley Fill Issues in the Little Coal River Watershed, West Virginia.* Keystone, CO: Keystone Center.

Appalachia Rising. 2010. "Mobilize to End Mountaintop Removal." Quoted in Scott Parkin. 2010. "Appalachia Rising: Mobilize to End Mountaintop Removal." *The Understory,* June 15. http://understory.ran.org/2010/06/15/appalachia-rising-mobilize-to -end-mountaintop-removalseptember-25---27-2010-washington-dc/.

Aurora Lights. N.d. *Journey Up Coal River: A Project of Aurora Lights.* auroralights.org /map_project/.

Barry, Joyce M. 2012. *Standing Our Ground: Women, Environmental Justice, and the Fight to End Mountaintop Removal.* Ohio University Press Series in Race, Ethnicity, and Gender in Appalachia. Athens: Ohio University Press.

Bean, Martha, Larry Fisher, and Mike Eng. 2007. "Assessment in Environmental and Public Policy Conflict Resolution: Emerging Theory, Patterns of Practice, and a Conceptual Framework." *Conflict Resolution Quarterly* 24 (4): 22.

Biggers, Jeff. 2006. *The United States of Appalachia: How Southern Mountaineers Brought Independence, Culture, and Enlightenment to America.* Emeryville, CA: Shoemaker and Hoard.

Biskupic, Joan. 2009. "Supreme Court Case with the Feel of a Best Seller." *USA Today,* February 16.

Black, Brian. 2011. "A Legacy of Extraction: Ethics in the Energy Landscape of Appalachia." In *Mountains of Injustice: Social and Environmental Justice in Appalachia,* edited by Michele Morrone and Geoffrey L. Buckley. Athens: Ohio University Press.

Blumm, Michael C., and D. Bernard Zaleha. 1989. "Federal Wetlands Protection under the Clean Water Act: Regulatory Ambivalence, Intergovernmental Tension, and a Call for Reform." *University of Colorado Law Review* 60 (4): 695–732.

Bragg v. Robertson. 1999. In F. Supp. 2d: S.D. W.VA.

Browand, Nathaniel. 2004. "Shifting the Boundary between the Sections 402 and 404 Permitting Programs by Expanding the Definition of Fill Material." *Boston College Environmental Affairs Law Review* 31 (3): 617–47.

Brisbin, Richard A., Jr. 2002. *A Strike Like No Other Strike: Law and Resistance during the Pittston Coal Strike of 1989–1990.* Baltimore: Johns Hopkins University Press.

Buckley, Geoffrey L. 2004. *Extracting Appalachia: Images of the Consolidation Coal Company, 1910-1945.* Athens: Ohio University Press.

Buckley, Geoffrey L., and Laura Allen. 2011. "Stories about Mountaintop Removal in the Appalachian Coalfields." In *Mountains of Injustice: Social and Environmental Justice in Appalachia,* edited by Michele Morrone and Geoffrey L. Buckley. Athens: Ohio University Press.

Burgess, Heidi. 2004. "Parties to Intractable Conflict." http://www.beyondintractability .org /essay/parties.

Burns, Shirley Stewart. 2007. *Bringing Down the Mountains: The Impact of Mountaintop Removal Surface Coal Mining on Southern West Virginia Communities, 1970-2004.* Morgantown: West Virginia University Press.

Bush, Robert A. Baruch, and Joseph P. Folger. 1994. *The Promise of Mediation: Responding to Conflict through Empowerment and Recognition.* Jossey-Bass Conflict Resolution Series. San Francisco: Jossey-Bass.

Byrd, Robert C. 2005. *Robert C. Byrd: Child of the Appalachian Coalfields.* Morgantown: West Virginia University Press.

Caskey, Antrim. 2010. "Dragline: Rock Creek." Appalachia Watch, www.appalachiawatch.org.

Caudill, Harry M. 1963. *Night Comes to the Cumberlands: A Biography of a Depressed Area.* Boston: Little, Brown.

Cavanaugh, Francine, and Adams Wood, dirs. 2010. *On Coal River.* New York: SnagFilms. DVD, 82 min.

Coal River Mountain, WV: Coal River Wind Project. 2008. Video. http://www.youtube.com /watch?v=39Ce7I6nXIw&feature=related.

Cooper, Dave. 2009. "Rocker Ted Nugent to Emcee Pro-Coal 'Friends of America' Rally in West Virginia." August 13. http://www.huffingtonpost.com/dave-cooper /rocker-ted-nugent-to-emce_b_258696.html.

CPCRI (Clinch-Powell Clean Rivers Initiative). 2007. "The Clinch-Powell Clean Rivers Initiative 2007 Symposium: Coal Mining and the Aquatic Environment." http:// vwrrc.vt.edu/cpcri/meetings_symposia.asp#Symposium07.

———. 2010. "Who We Are." http://vwrrc.vt.edu/cpcri/who_we_are.asp.

Dickinson, Tim. 2010. "The Eco-Warrior: Lisa Jackson's EPA." *Rolling Stone,* January 20, 34–37.

Drew, Christopher, and Richard Oppel Jr. 2009. "Mines to Mountaintops: Rewriting Coal Policy; Friends in the White House Come to Coal's Aid." *New York Times,* August 9, 1.

Duffy, Paul A. 2002. "How Filled Was My Valley: Continuing the Debate on Disposal Impacts." *Natural Resources and Environment* 17 (3): 143–45.

Dukes, E. Franklin. 2004. "What We Know about Environmental Conflict Resolution: An Analysis Based on Research." *Conflict Resolution Quarterly* 22 (1–2): 191–220.

———. 2007. "Rethinking Community Involvement for Superfund Site Reuse: The Case for Consensus-Building in Adaptive Management." In *Reclaiming the Land: Rethinking Superfund Institutions, Methods, and Practices,* edited by Gregg Macey and Jonathan Z. Cannon. New York: Springer.

Dukes, E. Franklin, Karen Firehock, and Juliana Birkhoff, eds. 2011. *Community-Based Collaboration: Bridging Socio-Ecological Research and Practice.* Charlottesville: University of Virginia Press.

Eilperin, Juliet. 2009. "EPA to Scrutinize Permits for Mountaintop-Removal Mining." *Washington Post*, March 25.

Eller, Ronald D. 1982. *Miners, Millhands, and Mountaineers: Industrialization of the Appalachian South, 1880–1930.* 1st ed. Twentieth-Century America Series. Knoxville: University of Tennessee Press.

———. 2008. *Uneven Ground: Appalachia since 1945.* Lexington: University Press of Kentucky.

EIA (US Energy Information Administration). 2012. "What Is the Role of Coal in the United States?" http://www.eia.gov/cfapps/energy_in_brief/role_coal_us.cfm.

———. 2013. "Annual Energy Outlook 2013." http://www.eia.gov/forecasts/aeo/pdf/0383(2013).pdf.

EPA (US Environmental Protection Agency). 2011a. "The Effects of Mountaintop Mines and Valley Fills on Aquatic Ecosystems of the Central Appalachian Coalfields." Washington, DC: Office of Research and Development, National Center for Environmental Assessment. http://cfpub.epa.gov/ncea/cfm/recordisplay.cfm?deid=225743.

———. 2011b. "EPA Halts Disposal of Mining Waste to Appalachian Waters at Proposed Spruce Mine." Press release, January 13, 2011. http://yosemite.epa.gov/opa/admpress.nsf/ec5b6cb1c087a230852573590040445/6b9ecfafebce79a585257817005 6a179!OpenDocument.

———. 2011c. "Final Determination of the US Environmental Protection Agency Concerning the Spruce No. 1 Mine." Washington, DC.

———. 2012. "Mid-Atlantic Mountaintop Mining." http://www.epa.gov/region03/mtntop/.

———. N.d. "Definitions of the Most Commonly Used Public Stakeholder Involvement Terms." http://www.epa.gov/stakeholders/definit.htm.

Evans, Sam. 2010. "Voices From the Desecrated Places: A Journey to End Mountaintop Removal Mining." *Harvard Environmental Law Review* 34 (2): 521–76.

Fagge, Roger. 1996. *Power, Culture, and Conflict in the Coalfields: West Virginia and South Wales, 1900–1922.* Manchester: Manchester University Press.

Fisher, Roger, and William Ury. 1983. *Getting to Yes: Negotiating Agreement without Giving In.* Edited by Bruce Patton. New York: Penguin Books.

Flaccavento, Anthony. 2010. "The Transition of Appalachia." *Solutions: For a Sustainable and Desirable Future* 1 (4): 34–44.

Freeman, Jordan. 2009. "Nationwide 21 Permit Hearing." Video. www.youtube.com/watch?v=EtwceseZz4w&feature=youtube_gdata.

Freese, Barbara. 2003. *Coal: A Human History.* New York: Penguin.

Fuschino, Julia. 2007. "Mountaintop Coal Mining and the Clean Water Act: The Fight Over Nationwide Permit 21." *Boston College Environmental Affairs Law Review* 34 (1): 179–207.

Galuszka, Peter A. 2012. *Thunder on the Mountain: Death at Massey and the Dirty Secrets behind Big Coal.* New York: St. Martin's.

Gaventa, John. 1980. *Power and Powerlessness: Quiescence and Rebellion in an Appalachian Valley*. Urbana: University of Illinois Press.

Geller, Phylis. 2009. *Coal Country*. Directed by Mari-Lynn Evans. Akron: Evening Star Productions.

Goodell, Jeff. 2006. *Big Coal: The Dirty Secret Behind America's Energy Future*. Boston: Houghton Mifflin.

Goodman, Amy. 2010. "'We are tearing down our mountains': Photojournalist Antrim Caskey on West Virginia's Fight against Mountaintop Removal Coal Mining." *Democracy Now*, March 31.

Hamill, Sean D. 2010. "W. Va. Churches Taking 'Hard Walk' on Mining." *Pittsburgh Post-Gazette*, August 8. http://www.democracynow.org/2010/3/31/we_are_tearing _down_our_mountains.

Haney, Bill, and Peter Rhodes. 2011. *The Last Mountain*. Directed by Haney. DVD. New York: New Video Group.

Headley, Terry L. 2010. "Concerning EPA's Proposed Revocation of the Spruce Mine Permit." http://www.friendsofcoal.org/20100610251/latest-news/comments-regarding -the-spruce-mine-no-1-permit-revocations.html.

Holley, Joe. 2010. "Robert C. Byrd, 1917–2010: A Public Servant for the Ages." *Washington Post*, June 29, 1.

House, Silas, and Jason Howard. 2009. *Something's Rising: Appalachians Fighting Mountaintop Removal*. Lexington: University Press of Kentucky.

Hufford, Mary. 2001. "Landscape and History at the Headwaters of the Big Coal River Valley: An Overview." Manuscript. Library of Congress, Washington, DC. http:// memory.loc.gov/ammem/collections/tending/essay5.pdf.

———. 2003. *Waging Democracy in the Kingdom of Coal: OVEC and the Movement for Social and Environmental Justice in Central Appalachia, 2002–2003*. Philadelphia: Center for Folklore and Ethnography, University of Pennsylvania.

HuntingtonNews.net. 2009. "NC Concert Headlined by WV Native Kathy Mattea Funds Campaign for Replacement of WV School below Coal Sludge Dam, Promotes Clean Energy." http://archives.huntingtonnews.net/state/090603-staff -statekathymattea.html.

IEED (Office of Indian Energy and Economic Development). 2012. "Coal Mining Technologies." http://www.teeic.anl.gov/er/coal/restech/index.cfm.

iLoveMountains. N.d. "What's My Connection to Mountaintop Removal?" http:// ilovemountains.org/my-connection.

Innes, Judith. 1999. "Evaluating Consensus Building." In *The Consensus Building Handbook: A Comprehensive Guide to Reaching Agreement*, edited by Lawrence Susskind, Sarah McKearnan, and Jennifer Thomas-Larmer, 631–78. Thousand Oaks, CA: Sage.

IPL (Interfaith Power and Light). N.d. "Public Policy: Coal." interfaithpowerandlight .org/public-policy/.

Koss, Geof, and Pam Radtke Russell. 2012. "Running Low on Power." *Congressional Quarterly Weekly*, July 14. http://public.cq.com/docs/weeklyreport/weeklyreport -000004123220.html.

Leung, Rebecca. 2004. "A Toxic Cover-Up? Did Bush Administration Cover Up Environmental Disaster?" *60 Minutes*, April 1. http://www.cbsnews.com/news/a-toxic-cover-up/.

Lewicki, Roy J., Barbara Gray, and Michael Elliott, eds. 2003. *Making Sense of Intractable Environmental Conflicts: Frames and Cases*. Washington, DC: Island Press.

Lewis, Ronald L. 1998. *Transforming the Appalachian Countryside: Railroads, Deforestation, and Social Change in West Virginia, 1880–1920*. Chapel Hill: University of North Carolina Press.

Loeb, Penny. 2007. *Moving Mountains: How One Woman and Her Community Won Justice From Big Coal*. Lexington: University Press of Kentucky.

McGinley, Patrick. 2004. "From Pick and Shovel to Mountaintop Removal: Environmental Injustice in the Appalachian Coalfields." *Environmental Law* 34 (1): 21–106.

McIlmoil, Rory, and Evan Hansen. 2010. *The Decline of Central Appalachian Coal and the Need for Economic Diversification*. Morgantown, WV: Downstream Strategies. http://www.downstreamstrategies.com/exp_pubs_reports.htm.

Mitchell, Timothy. 2009. "Carbon Democracy." *Economy and Society* 38 (3): 399–432.

———. 2013. *Carbon Democracy: Political Power in the Age of Oil*. London: Verso.

Montrie, Chad. 2003. *To Save the Land and People: A History of Opposition to Surface Coal Mining in Appalachia*. Chapel Hill: University of North Carolina Press.

———. 2011. "'We mean to stop them, one way or another': Coal, Power, and the Fight against Strip Mining in Appalachia." In *Mountains of Injustice: Social and Environmental Justice in Appalachia*, edited by Michele Morrone and Geoffrey L. Buckley. Athens: Ohio University Press.

Morrone, Michele, and Geoffrey L. Buckley, eds. 2011. *Mountains of Injustice: Social and Environmental Justice in Appalachia*. Athens: Ohio University Press.

Moyers, Bill. 2007. "Mountaintop Mining Update." *Bill Moyers' Journal*, September 7. http://www.pbs.org/moyers/journal/09072007/watch3.html.

Mulkern, Anne C. 2010. "Lobbying: Coal Ad Blitz Launches New Spot as Industry Sees Political Gains." http://www.eenews.net/stories/87373.

NIOT. 2009. *Not in Our Town*. http://www.niot.org/patrice-oneill.

NMA (National Mining Association). 2010. *Stand Up for American Coal Jobs DC Rally 2010*. Video. http://www.youtube.com/watch?v=OvMuLID1hEo.

O'Brien, Soledad. 2011. *Battle for Blair Mountain: Working in America*. CNN. August 14.

O'Leary, Sean, and Ted Boettner. 2011. *Booms and Busts: The Impact of West Virginia's Energy Economy*. Charleston: West Virginia Center on Budget and Policy.

Osha, Jen. 2010. "The Power-Knowledge to Move Mountains: Subaltern Discourses of Mountaintop Removal in Coal River Valley, West Virginia." PhD diss., West Virginia University, Morgantown.

OVEC (Ohio Valley Environmental Coalition). 2010a. "Coalfield Residents and Scientists Meet with Governor." *Winds of Change*, March. http://ohvec.org/newsletters/woc_2010_03/index.html.

———. 2010b. "Meeting with the Governor and Kathy Mattea." *Winds of Change*, March. http://www.ohvec.org/newsletters/woc_2010_03/article_18.html.

Palmer, M. A., E. S. Bernhardt, W. H. Schlesinger, K. N. Eshleman, E. Foufoula-Georgiou, M. S. Hendryx, A. D. Lemly, G. E. Likens, O. L. Loucks, M. E. Power, P. S. White, P. R. Wilcock 2010. "Mountaintop Mining Consequences." *Science* 327 (5962): 148–49.

PCSD (President's Council on Sustainable Development). 1997. *Sustainable America—A New Consensus for Prosperity, Opportunity, and a Healthy Environment for the Future.* Washington, DC. http://clinton2.nara.gov/PCSD/Publications/TF_Reports/amertop.html

Pruitt, Dean, Jeffrey Rubin, and Sung Hee Kim. 2003. *Social Conflict: Escalation, Stalemate, and Settlement.* New York: McGraw-Hill.

Quillen, Michael J. 2010. "Interview with Michael J. Quillen of Alpha Natural Resources." By *Virginia News*, October 28. http://www.virginiabusiness.com/news/article/interview-with-michael-j.-quillen-chairman-alpha-natural-resources-inc.

Raz, Guy, and Lauren Silverman. 2011. "Miners Weather the Slow Burn of Coal's Demise." *All Things Considered*, National Public Radio, July 14. http://www.npr.org/2012/07/14/156784701/miners-weather-the-slow-burn-of-coals-demise.

Reece, Erik. 2006. *Lost Mountain: A Year in the Vanishing Wilderness: Radical Strip Mining and the Devastation of Appalachia.* New York: Riverhead Books.

Reid, Bill. 2010. "Corps Suspends Nationwide Permit 21." *Coal News: Coal's Foremost Publication* 7 (7): 1.

Roberts, Cecil. 2008. Letter to UMWA Surface Mining Members, April 8. http://www.umwa.org/?q=news/cecil-roberts-letter-umwa-surface-mining-members.

Rockefeller, Jay. 2012a. "Floor Statement on Inhofe Resolution of Disapproval," June 20. http://www.rockefeller.senate.gov/public/index.cfm/floor-statements?ID=23709dde-73bc-4377-ac1a-0bc051d83449.

———. 2012b. Press release: "Rockefeller Statement on Inhofe Resolution Vote," June 20. http://www.rockefeller.senate.gov/public/index.cfm/press-releases?ID=f39e2234-33d6-4cb4-857a-18466b3c5a29.

Sayles, John. 1987. *Matewan*. Directed by Sayles. Cinecom International Films.

Scarbro, Lorelei. 2009. "Climate Hero Lorelei Scarbro: An Appalachian Grandmother Says No to Coal, Yes to Wind Power." Inteview by Kate Sheppard. *Yes! Magazine*, November 10. http://www.yesmagazine.org/issues/climate-action/climate-hero-lorelei-scarbro.

———. 2010. "We Don't Live Where They Mine, They Mine Where We Live." http://www.interfaithpowerandlight.org/2010/06/lorelei-scarbro-we-dont-live-where-they-mine-they-mine-where-we-live/.

Scott, Rebecca R. 2010. *Removing Mountains: Extracting Nature and Identity in the Appalachian Coalfields.* Minneapolis: University of Minnesota Press.

Shapiro, Tricia. 2010. *Mountain Justice: Homegrown Resistance to Mountaintop Removal, for the Future of Us All.* Oakland: AK Press.

Shifflett, Crandall A. 1991. *Coal Towns: Life, Work, and Culture in Company Towns of Southern Appalachia, 1880–1960.* 1st ed. Knoxville: University of Tennessee Press.

Shnayerson, Michael. 2006. "The Rape of Appalachia." *Vanity Fair*, May.

———. 2008. *Coal River*. New York: Farrar, Straus and Giroux.

Shogan, Robert. 2004. *The Battle of Blair Mountain: The Story of America's Largest Labor Uprising.* Boulder: Westview.

Sierra Club. N.d. "Beyond Coal," beyondcoal.org.

Spangler, Brad. 2003. "Stakeholder Representatives." *Beyond Intractability.* November. http://www.beyondintractability.org/essay/stakeholder.

Stern, Gerald M. 2008. *The Buffalo Creek Disaster: How the Survivors of One of the Worst Disasters in Coal-Mining History Brought Suit against the Coal Company—and Won.* New York: Vintage Books.

Stephens, Beth, and Annie Sprinkle, dirs. 2013. *Goodbye Gauley Mountain: An Ecosexual Love Story.* Film.

Susskind, Lawrence, and Jennifer Thomas-Larmer. 1999. "Conducting a Conflict Assessment." In *The Consensus Building Handbook: A Comprehensive Guide to Reaching Agreement,* edited by Lawrence Susskind, Sarah McKearnan, and Jennifer Thomas-Larmer, 99–136. Thousand Oaks, CA: Sage.

Tams, W. P., Jr. 2001. *The Smokeless Coal Fields of West Virginia: A Brief History.* Morgantown: West Virginia University Press.

Thomas, Jerry Bruce. 1998. *An Appalachian New Deal: West Virginia in the Great Depression.* Lexington: University Press of Kentucky.

UMWA (United Mine Workers of America). "Surface Coal Mining." http://www.umwa.org/?q=content/surface-coal-mining.

USACE (US Army Corps of Engineers). 2009. "Army Corps of Engineers to Hold Public Hearings on Two Proposals Related to Nationwide Permit 21 in the Appalachian Region." September 10. http://www.lrl.usace.army.mil/Media/NewsStories/tabid/10554/Article/7801/.

———. 2010. "Suspension of Nationwide Permit 21." *Federal Register.* Washington, DC. http://www.federalregister.gov/articles/2010/06/18/2010-14778/suspension-of-nationwide-permit-21.

USACE, DOI, and EPA (US Department of the Army, US Department of the Interior, and US Environmental Protection Agency). 2009. "Implementing the Interagency Action Plan on Appalachian Surface Coal Mining," Memorandum of Understanding. Washington, DC. http://water.epa.gov/lawsregs/guidance/wetlands/upload/2009_06_10_wetlands_pdf_Final_MTM_MOU_6-11-09.pdf.

USIP (US Institute of Peace). 2007. *Natural Resources, Conflict, and Conflict Resolution.* Washington, DC: USIP.

Vuranch, Karen. N.d. "Coal Camp Memories: Curriculum." http://www.coalcampmemories.com.

Ward, Ken, Jr. 2009a. "Corps to Hold Hearings on Streamlined MTR Permits." *Coal Tattoo: Mining's Mark on Our World.* Blog, September 11. http://blogs.wvgazette.com/coaltattoo/2009/09/11/.

———. 2009b. "Sen. Byrd: 'Coal Must Embrace the Future.'" *Coal Tattoo: Mining's Mark on Our World.* Blog, December 3. http://blogs.wvgazette.com/coaltattoo/2009/12/03/sen-byrd-coal-must-embrace-the-future/.

———. 2010a. "Manchin Calls for Calm in the Coalfields." *Coal Tattoo: Mining's Mark on Our World.* Blog, January 25. http://blogs.wvgazette.com/coaltattoo/2010/01/25/.

———. 2010b. "Over the Years, Byrd Evolved on Coal Stance." *Charleston (WV) Gazette*, June 28. http://www.wvgazette.com/News/201006280502.

———. 2012a. *Coal Tattoo: Mining's Mark on Our World*. Blog. *Charleston (WV) Gazette*. http:// blogs.wvgazette.com/coaltattoo.

———. 2012b. "New Data Reflects Coal Layoffs, but No Job Collapse." *Charleston (WV) Gazette*. August 8. http://www.wvgazette.com/News/201208080279.

———. 2012c. "Rockefeller Calls on Coal Industry to Stop 'Scare Tactics.'" *Charleston (WV) Gazette*, June 20. http://www.wvgazette.com/News/201206200049.

———. 2012d. "War Is War: Why Not Call Coal Debate Something Else?" *Coal Tattoo: Mining's Mark on Our World*. Blog, July 27. http://blogs.wvgazette.com/coaltattoo /2012/07/27/.

Warrick, Joby. 2004. "Appalachia Is Paying Price for White House Rule Change." *Washington Post*. August 17. http://www.washingtonpost.com/wp-dyn/articles /A6462-2004Aug16.html.

Werschkul, Ben, dir. 2010. *A Fight for a Mountaintop*. Video. http://www.nytimes.com /video/business/1247468621885/a-fight-for-a-mountaintop.html.

Williams, John Alexander. 2002. *Appalachia: A History*. Chapel Hill: University of North Carolina Press.

Wondolleck, Julia, Barbara Gray, and Todd Bryan. 2003. "Us versus Them: How Identities and Characterizations Influence Conflict." *Environmental Practice* 5 (3): 207–13.

INDEX

Italic numbers refer to pages with illustrations.